The Mystique of Love Unveiled

The Mystique of Love Unveiled

How to Take Control of Your Love Life

L.K. MICKELSON

Cassandra Publications
Loveland, Colorado

ISBN-13: 978-0-9727527-1-8
ISBN-10: 0-972-7527-1-4

Library of Congress Control Number: 2005939003

Printed in the United States of America
10 9 8 7 6 5 4 3 2 1

Interior and cover design by To The Point Solutions
www.tothepointsolutions.com

To my dear and treasured mother.
I have never doubted her love for me.

CONTENTS

Contents

Acknowledgments

TO MY MANY FRIENDS AND RELATIVES WHO HAVE ENCOURAGED me to complete this project: some of whom reached the point where they became rather pesky (since I have been working on the book for three years).

To Darrell and Louise Jansa, Kathy Harris, and Elizabeth McCoy, who not only encouraged me but also found value in the concepts contained herein.

To my constant companions, John Stouffer and Charles Demander: these gentlemen debated with me for endless hours and thus managed to keep my focus on the target. They were the biggest pests of all.

To my able assistants, Deborah Lehman and Christy Crites. Their appreciation of my ideas was invaluable to me just when I needed it. They encouraged me by making me feel as if what I had to say was important and needed to be published.

To two extra-special young ladies—my sweet stepdaughters; Alanna and Shawna Riley. To Alanna I owe my eye-catching cover; designed when she was only eighteen years old.

To her younger sister Shawna, who not only wrote the poem that introduces the book but who also bravely contemplated these concepts and gave me superb feedback from the younger crowd.

And to Nancy Mickelson, whose talent and skills put the final touches on the book, including the title.

Finally, I acknowledge my editor, Mary Jo Zazueta, for her input and guidance. There is no doubt this book would be entirely different without her advice. I had, in fact, nearly published a different version, but she had the courage to discourage me, so I redid the entire project.

Love

The stranger you know
Who fills you with bliss
While taking away
All happiness

Feeling so free
A bird in a cage
Growing younger
As you age

Confused as you are
It seems to make sense
Thoughts are too strong
Feelings so intense

Hard to gain
Even harder when lost
Emotion's full price
At half the cost

Love

SHAWNA RILEY

"If one judges love by its effects, it resembles hate more than affection."

~ *Ovid*

"I HATE HIM! I HATE HIM! I HATE HIM!" THESE WORDS GUSHED out with an intensity that left no doubt about the woman's feelings. She was an acquaintance of mine, whose husband had inexplicably filed for divorce. The divorce papers arrived without warning or explanation.

Believing she truly meant what she said, I responded in support, "Well, if that's the case, then I guess it's good riddance to bad rubbish. Right?"

"What do you mean by that?" she replied in disbelief. "No-o. I don't want him to leave. I love him so much I don't think I can live without him."

"But didn't you just say you hated him?" I asked in surprise.

"Yes, but I think what I meant to say was that I'm angry and upset with him. How could he do this to me? All I do is cry all day and I've been so depressed I can't even function at work. I just want him to come back to me. I'll forgive him for everything if he'll just come back," she sobbed.

"Wait just a minute here," I demanded. "Haven't you been complaining about the fact that all the two of you ever do is fight when you're together? Didn't you tell me last week that you were thinking of leaving him?"

"I know, and I'll admit I said that, but I wasn't really serious. Where will I go? What will I do? I feel so lost and confused. I'd give anything to just have him back and return to the life we had together. Can't he see how much I still love him?"

This conversation has been played out perhaps millions of times in the game of love; a game so confusing that these conversations can last for hours on end, with no real conclusions being reached because the whole business of love is contradictory and confusing.

This book is about the confusing feelings we experience before, during, and after we fall in love. I have three goals: to make you laugh, to make you cry, but mostly to make you think.

Much has been written about love; volumes, in fact. Yet in spite of its popularity as a subject, we still know very little about what love really is. Numerous and varied intellectual disciplines have provided their own definitions—resulting in a few general agreements—yet there remains a wide disparity of opinion and no acceptable conclusions have been reached. Philosophers, theologians, psychologists, and scientists see love from their limited perspectives with each merely adding to the intellectual quagmire. Even more confusing is the fact that men view love much differently than women. And, to make matters worse, Hollywood puts its two cents worth into the fray and we end up with so much confusion no one has any idea what to believe. It's a mess. Truly a mess.

This book was written to *challenge nearly everything you hold to be true about love*. I believe that many of the current facts about love are so far off the mark that millions of people are making enormous mistakes because of those beliefs. People marry and divorce because of certain truisms about love that turn out to be false. We are naïve in thinking we can live by the current doctrines of love. Love as a concept and a belief system is one huge, massive, social and personal form of self-deception. I sincerely believe there is a better, healthier way for us to view love.

If there is such a thing as love, perhaps locating, defining, and limiting it will prove to be beneficial to all of us. As it stands, too many of the accepted beliefs run contrary to our human nature. Exposing the truths and disposing of the myths will open the doors to realistic discussions and practical expectations.

We have all come to expect so much from *love* that it has taken on a near mystical aura. We get glassy-eyed just thinking about it. A great love story makes all of us cry (which we enjoy doing), and, with each tear, love takes on an even more magical/mystical aura. The tears seem to empower love to a near supernatural level.

Quotes and phrases about love are everywhere in our daily lives—in the lyrics of songs and in sermons in church. "Love is all that really matters in life," maintains one group. "God is love," adds another. Love is_____; love is____; love is_____. Bartlett's book of famous quotations is full of these love is 'ums.

This book will add a *practical* perspective to the discussion of love. Love is not the end-all to life. Love isn't magical, mystical, or supernatural and, in fact, for survival reasons, it is especially one-sided and selfish. However, and I emphasize, once love is understood, there is nothing more beautiful in life.

A New View

The conclusions I reach in this book differ greatly from other books written on the subject. Some conclusions may even irritate you because they are so different from the norm—but I hope you will read through to the end. Perhaps something will strike a cord and make sense to you—something that will enhance your personal relationships and make them more successful.

While some of the ideas will be controversial, perhaps that is the beauty of it. Any theory or idea of value should promote thought, reflection, research and discussion—thereby making a difference in people's lives. Theories are also valuable when they succeed in predicting some event or behavior. This book should do both.

All our young lives we search for someone to love . . . someone who makes us complete. We choose partners and change partners. We dance to a song of heartbreak and hope. All the while wondering if somewhere, somehow, there's someone perfect . . . who might be searching for us.

From *The Wonder Years*

Author's note: This book will not be written from either the feminine or masculine point of view. The English language is extremely awkward in this regard. So whenever the contents seem to apply only to one or the other, a simple reversal of roles will make them applicable to both sexes. I don't wish to always be writing he/she and him/her when truthfully grammarians recommend the use of the masculine gender.

CHAPTER 1

The Problem With Love: How It Causes Such Misery

"You love her, but she loves him, and he loves somebody else...you just can't win. And so it goes till the day you die, this thing they call love...it's gonna make you cry... Love stinks. Yeah, yeah, love stinks"

~ J. Geils Band

I HATE TO ADMIT THIS, BUT THE FIRST TIME MY HEART WAS broken I nearly lost my mind. Even though it happened decades ago, when I was a teenager, I can vividly recall how awful I felt. I cried extensively, played love songs on my stereo endlessly, turned into a consummate grouch socially, became totally unbearable at home, and even contemplated suicide.

My girlfriend had dumped me and no matter what I said or did she wouldn't change her mind and come back to me. Thus, it seems, I went temporarily insane. Although it's funny now, at the time I was a bit too overwrought for my own good. For several years afterward, I mourned her loss and never doubted for one minute that I still loved her—deeply. Mine was a special kind of love–different from everyone else's. Truly, only I loved so completely and intensely. Thus, no one could possibly understand how I felt.

Even my suicidal fantasies were created in order to prove to her and others how much I loved her. I actually visualized my funeral, where grieving family and friends would finally realize how extra special my love had been and that, indeed, no one on earth had ever loved another more than I had loved her. I hoped they felt guilty about ever questioning my love. *Ah, yes! Those were the good old days!*

Fortunately, I survived; which is amazing considering how utterly depressed I was. I learned the hard way how dreadful heartbreak feels. I'm not exaggerating when I say I mooned over that girl for years. It didn't matter that I had completely lost track of her and what she was doing with her life. I always hoped to get back with her at some time in the future. I marvel now at the life-changing power and duration of the feelings I had about that event in my life. *Isn't love something?*

After graduating from college, I taught psychology in high school. When I noticed one of my students going through the same thing I had experienced, I asked her to stay after school and talk with me. I was able to empathize with her and reassure her that she would come through this time of trial; that she was not alone in her suffering. We talked for hours and she too somehow survived.

Once I knew my terrible experience hadn't been endured in vain, I realized I could help others by explaining what I had discovered. I thus began to ponder the mysteries of love in earnest. My main questions were simply: why in the Sam hell (one of my father's favorite expressions) do people react to romantic difficulties in such an inexplicable fashion? Why, also, do our bodies make us feel so completely miserable? What is going on inside us when we feel so distraught? Finally, and perhaps most importantly; are these feelings genuine signs and proofs of love? Is this how we know we are in love with someone—when we are ready to jump off a cliff because we have lost them? What sort of insanity is that? Should love, "glorious love," be so destructive to our well-being?

There is a societal understanding, of sorts, that proposes that the crazier one acts when faced with loss of a romantic relationship, the more he/she is considered to be "in love." Why is that? Surely love, by definition, should be a positive experience. In fact, poets often use the word *bliss* to describe feelings associated with love. Why then, would anguish prove anything?

It is easy to conclude that love is a mystery and thereby ignore the entire dilemma—but that's just not possible—not for me anyway. Many of life's major decisions are made directly or indirectly because of love. Sadly, some of those decisions are wrong. Consider how many bad marriages there have been because the meaning of love was misunderstood. Some of those marriages were doomed from the start.

It's tempting to say: "Oh well! No harm done. Live and learn. Life goes on." But the consequences of bad marriages often prove to be devastating, both emotionally and financially. For instance, there are millions of single parents raising children alone because their marriages failed. The battles over what it means to love someone leave everyone totally confused—especially the children caught in the middle.

Consider, too, how much violence is connected with love. People actually kill others because their feelings are so intense and unbearable. Many others kill themselves. After years of dealing with teenagers, I concluded that most teenage suicides are somehow connected to problems with love relationships.

> Consider how many bad marriages there have been because love was misunderstood.

Whether we like to admit it or not, much of the advice being given to distraught lovers is not helpful. Telling these unfortunates to "just get over it," or "the hurt will go away soon enough"—is useless. Absolutely useless! There doesn't appear to be any immediate cure for the malady of heartbreak and yet it is, perhaps, the most devastating of all emotions.

I liken the feelings of heartbreak to the feelings a soldier experiences during mortal combat. Both instances involve extreme emotions and inescapable situations. Whether under siege from enemy fire or abandoned and rejected by an adored person, the individual has no control over what is going on. This lack of control creates long-term emotional states that cause feelings of helplessness and despair.

That's why this book has been written: to explain love and other emotions so as to help the reader understand the myriad feelings people experience in the process of falling in and out of love. The challenge is to clarify the concept of "love" in such a way that it no longer confuses or causes misery to those who do love. This book will walk you through the steps to understanding love and preventing heartbreak, so you'll be enlightened and your life will be enriched. I hope you enjoy the journey.

Daniel: Tell her then.
Sam (ten years old): Tell her what?
Daniel: Tell her that you love her.
Sam: No way! Anyway, they fly tonight.
Daniel: Even better! Sam—you've got nothing to lose, and you'll always regret it if you don't. I never told your mom enough. I should have told her every day because she was perfect every day.
Sam: Okay, Dad! Let's do it! Let' s go get the shit kicked out of us by love.

From the movie *Love, Actually*

CHAPTER 2

Love's Confusion:
Are You in Love? Are You Sure?

"There is no pleasure like the pain of being loved and loving."

~ W. M. PRAED, *Legend of the Haunted Tree*

IF LOVE IS A REALITY, THEN COMMON SENSE DICTATES IT MUST be definable. However, finding a definition is difficult. Everyone, it seems, has his own definition. I prefer this one: I simply connect the word *love* with the word *pleasure*. Love as pleasure is the *only* definition I find acceptable. Obviously this is the first step toward viewing love from a practical perspective—one that tries to remove the abstractions and fantastical expectations associated with it.

With this approach, *anything that pleases you can be loved.* A person can love chocolate, skiing, a pet, and even a new ballpoint pen. Thus, with respect to human relationships, the ultimate love would be felt for the person who pleases you the most. Using this definition, one could come up with a formula for love with the intensity of love being directly proportional to the amount of pleasure being derived from the love object (whether the love object is a person, thing, or activity).

This definition of love appeals to me because it is the least confusing. You could rate all the things you love on a scale and thus decide what (or whom) you love the most. Things you own could be rated according to the pleasure derived from them. You may find, in your hierarchy of loves, you get the most pleasure from your boat, then your car, house, stereo, etc., in descending order.

This scale isn't overly impressive if you are dealing with objects, but what about the *people* scale? According to the formula, the people you love the most should also give you the most pleasure. Make sense? Sure it does! People who show pleasing behavior toward you are lovable to some degree. You could rate each person you know on this "scale of lovability" just as you rated your material objects. If you love logically, the result should be that the person who pleases you the most is also loved by you the most; and, vice versa, the person who pleases you the least is loved least.

A few facts based on this definition of love:

1. Lovable people show pleasing behavior toward others.
2. If you want to be lovable, you must please others.
3. If you love someone and desire to prove your love, you must do more to please that individual.

And, in the reverse:

4. People who are not pleasing to others are not lovable to the degree that they are displeasing.
5. Aggression of any sort has no place in love.

The above facts simplify love. *If it could only be that simple!* Unfortunately, in the final analysis, there are many objections to this definition.

Aggression

Sometimes two people who are in love act unpleasantly and aggressively toward each other. Often the aggression is unbelievably vicious! I once observed a couple having a knock-down, drag-out fight, during which they hit and kicked each other mercilessly until bystanders broke them apart and hauled him out the door. The ludicrous part was, as he was being taken away, (by the police), she, while being restrained by friends, was screaming at him—not hateful words, as one might expect, but words that expressed intense love. She yelled a classic farewell at the top of her lungs: "I love you, you son of a bitch!"

What is the reality in this case? Does she love him or hate him? Who is to say? Her closest friend may feel sorry for her and, perhaps, conclude that she truly does love him—too much for her own good. A stranger might say that she just *thinks* she loves him, when in reality, she doesn't. Perhaps she needs to get away from him for a while.

To carry this line of reasoning further (for the fun of it), suppose we were to ask a psychologist, whose analysis might be more profound, for an opinion. Try this one on for size: "The love that is felt by this young woman is actually an unconscious expression of her love for her deceased father, whom she loved intensely. The new lover, or lover surrogate, actually symbolizes the relationship she had with her father. When her father was alive, however, she was prohibited from expressing this love because of an overly jealous mother who saw her daughter as a competitor for her husband's affection," etc., *ad absurdum*! (That's Latin for "Things get really stupid from here on.")

Do I have the answer to the riddle? I think so. The problem lies in our use of the word *love*. What this woman is feeling should not be called *love*.

Pleasure

Another objection focuses on the word *pleasure*. With this objection the critic points out that what is pleasurable to one person is not necessarily pleasurable to another; therefore, we can't define love as only being pleasure related unless we find a universal definition of pleasure.

There is much truth in this objection; but from a scientific perspective, pleasure can best be understood as it relates to the survival of an organism. Things in the environment that are pleasurable to humans have "survival value" of some sort. Similarly, things in the environment that are painful usually signal that our survival is being threatened. Our ancestors determined what things had survival value and what things didn't using this method of sorting. This "species learning" has become part of our genetic structure through the process of natural selection. At birth this "genetic survival lesson" is combined with "social survival lessons," resulting in a road map to survival in a particular culture.

An example of pleasure as related to genetic survival can be found in the experience of skin-to-skin contact between humans. With few exceptions, humans seek physical contact with other humans. This genetic survival lesson has obvious value for the species. Through natural selection, members of the human species who did not derive pleasure from skin-to-skin contact died off without reproducing. Those who did receive pleasure from this contact were more likely to reproduce and pass on this pleasure-seeking trait to future generations.

Other genetic pleasures followed a similar development (eating, sleeping, etc.). As a consequence, there is almost universal agreement among people concerning what is pleasurable and what isn't. Only cultural influences can account for various pleasure preferences (social survival lessons).

Even if we acknowledge that what is socially pleasurable for one person is not necessarily pleasurable for another, there is still some general agreement. Certain things in the environment are universally accepted as being pleasurable, for instance, good food, warm sun, great music, etc. Likewise, people view certain kinds of human behavior—companionship, stimulating conversation, kind words, touch etc., as being pleasurable.

Love is sharing life's pleasures with another. Love is the laughing, talking, joking, playing, communicating, and sharing that enhances the relationships we have with others. Love *does* make life worth living. Love is directly connected to all of the good times in life.

Words can actually cause feelings and the word *love* does just that. Love has been associated with pleasure so successfully that it actually causes people to feel good. Plus, love is also tied with other words that can cause similar positive feelings.

To take this point a little further: One reason our culture values the word love is that *all the pleasures of life are connected with the word*. Therefore, any objections to love appear to be objections to these pleasures as well.

For example, words like *touch, cuddle, fondle, mother, baby,* and *sunshine* have the ability to arouse feelings. In movies, this fact has been used to create and manipulate the audience's feelings. Each time a director wants the audience to feel love he somehow connects it with other powerful words and images.

> Love is sharing life's pleasures with another.

Numerous movies have scenes with two lovers frolicking through fields of flowers under the warm rays of the sun, kissing and holding hands, etc. The point is—the flowers and sunshine are what really cause the pleasure—without the need for the word *love*. The kissing causes the pleasure—not the word *love*. Love acquires its magic from those other words, actions, and images.

The Feelings of Love

Some people argue that love goes *beyond pleasure*. They believe the pleasure one receives from a love relationship is only secondary. What one person *feels* toward another is the most important aspect of love; therefore, any definition of love that leaves out feelings is incomplete. Otherwise, how does one explain the phenomenon whereby a person experiences intense love for an absent lover, even though no pleasure is being directly obtained from him?

These people maintain that there is more to love than pleasure. Feelings are of greater importance. Love is an emotion (a feeling) and without that emotion there is no true love.

This objection is critical to the concepts in this book because at its heart are society's views of emotions themselves. For some reason we, as a society, value all emotions and feelings even when they are *not* pleasurable. Thus, even when love *hurts*, it is still love.

Perhaps the pain people all too often refer to as being love simply involves the loss of pleasure (survival needs). This loss results in bad feelings—ones the individual cannot ignore. We mistakenly call these bad feelings proof that we love.

Classically, one of the best indicators we are in love is provided by how awful we feel whenever we lose that love. We believe the resulting bad feelings prove we are in love. (It sure proved it to me as a naïve teenager. If anyone had suggested that my feelings were not love, I would have scoffed at such foolishness. I knew I was in love—the pain was my proof.)

I Love You Today

I recently began to pay close attention to the various times people say "I love you." I have narrowed those occasions down to four distinct circumstances. I will refer to them as the four types of love. They are: Sexual Love, Attachment Love, Intellectual Love, and Emotional Love. These four types of love help to clarify *why* love is being expressed at any given time.

In each circumstance, saying "I love you" is socially acceptable and expected. For example, when we find ourselves feeling especially affectionate toward someone (Attachment Love), we are inclined to tell that individual we love him. If a romantic attachment (Sexual Love) is involved, we might go further and say we are "in love" with him. We say "I love you" to a lifelong soul mate simply because he makes us feel content (Intellectual Love). Finally "I love you" is expressed whenever we fear losing someone we deem important to us (Emotional Love).

It's ok to laugh in the bedroom as long as you don't point.
Will Durst

CHAPTER 3

The Four Types of Love: What Makes Love Exciting

"How do I love thee? Let me count the ways."

~ Elizabeth Barrett Browning

I OWN A 54-VOLUME SET OF LITERARY *GREAT BOOKS* THAT contain thousands of years of philosophical, psychological, and religious writings. Throughout the set there is a major theme: an analysis of the behavior and feelings of mankind. Apparently, since the beginning of the written word, men have been trying to understand why we behave as we do. Interestingly, *love* and its synonyms take up a significant portion of the writings. Love has been a topic of discussion for eons.

After extensively reading these books, I have concluded that human beings really aren't that difficult to understand. In fact, I think it's fair to say that our behavior can be understood from the simple perspective of one word: *survival.* Mankind, whether individually or as a group, will do anything necessary to survive. Thus, instead of asking *why* someone behaves in a certain manner, it might be more appropriate to ask how certain behavior *helped him survive.* This idea becomes complicated simply because man has three classes of survival needs: physical, social, and psychological.

For example, rejection from a desired group of friends can cause one to believe that his survival has been threatened, resulting in numerous emotional reactions. Since feelings of rejection aren't always obvious to the casual observer, his resulting behavior might not appear to make sense. Subjectively, however, even suicide can make sense.

Based upon this approach, consider this introductory statement: *All behavior of man and other living organisms can be understood as a function of survival.*

This simple approach to life will help us understand love. As I mentioned earlier, the pleasures associated with love have survival value. So, too, do the pains.

This book follows a basic outline represented by the diagram below. As you can see in the diagram on the adjacent page, there are two separate types of survival to be considered: that of the species and that of the individual. As subcategories, there are the four types of love.

The human body is biologically designed to reproduce the species and to do whatever is necessary to keep the individual alive. Generally speaking, these two survival mechanisms work in harmony, although the types of behavior they cause can be quite different. Sometimes they operate in conflict with each other, especially when social norms attempt to dictate opposing behaviors. Thus, while coveting thy neighbor's wife may be a natural inclination, there are societal commandments against doing so.

On an individual level, whether talking about love or hunger, each of us interprets these primitively controlled feelings in order to decide how best to behave. More often than not, the primitive area of our brains (the part we share with other animal species) ends up controlling most of our behavior. Learning to transfer that control to the intellect is a better plan. Throughout history, several societies have worked hard to achieve this lofty goal. The stoic mannerisms of the British intellectual come to mind.

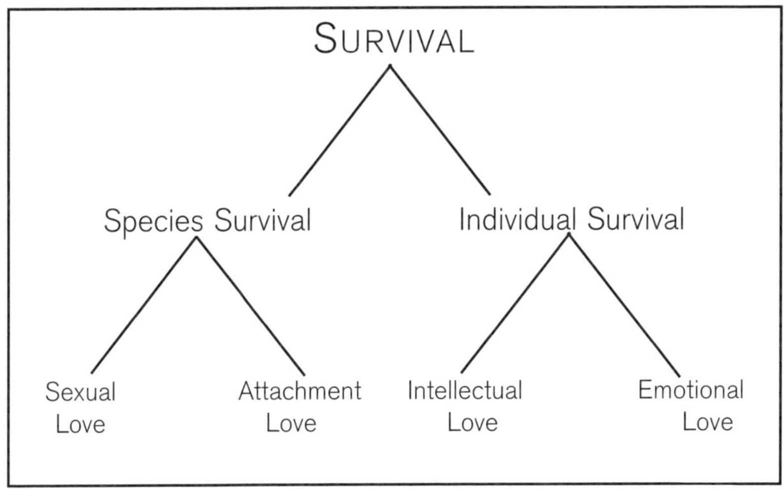

Perhaps we should learn to *ignore* much of that "emotional cacophony" and make decisions intellectually. I know this may sound dry and unexciting but—truthfully—the only significant difference between man and other animals lies in our intellect. The emotions and various other feelings we value so completely can easily cause us to make decisions that aren't in our own best interest.

If love is blind, why is lingerie so popular?
Jimmy Williams

Chapter 4

Sexual Love:
Is the Ecstasy of Sex Really Love?

"Men need sexual fulfillment in order to respond to a woman emotionally; women need emotional fulfillment to respond to a man sexually."

~ Ellen Krieg

I FIRST OBSERVED THE AWESOME POWER OF SEXUAL LOVE WHEN I was seven years old. There must have been a hundred kids in the neighborhood I grew up in—but there were even more dogs. Nearly every family had a dog; mine owned a Heinz-57 mutt that was allowed to run free, like most dogs in those days. One summer day, while I was playing with friends in the alley between the rows of houses in our development, a large pack of dogs turned into the alley and came running toward us. This was no ordinary pack either. This was a nasty, snarling, fighting pack of nearly insane canines. They were moving at a high rate of speed and fighting amongst themselves as they ran. It was certainly scary for a seven-year-old.

The lead dog was small and mild-mannered compared to the followers, ambling along as if out for a Sunday stroll—not involved or concerned about any of the fighting that raged amongst the rabble. But followers *she* had.

You probably guessed why: the leader, a female, was in heat and her admirers were fighting ferociously. Eventually, one member of the pack succeeded in winning the contest (perhaps this is where the term "lucky dog" comes from) causing the entire mob to stop its forward progress and begin milling around the loving couple. At that point, a half-dozen concerned parents got into the fray with water hoses, brooms, and such in an attempt to disperse the unlucky suitors—hoping to shield innocent eyes from the awkward scene. Truly, this would have made a great scene in a movie. The turmoil was unbelievable. It was quite exciting and made for a rather memorable afternoon.

I remember one other significant thing about that day—something I shall never forget. I was standing beside a friend when he looked up at his mother and asked what all those dogs were trying to do to the one little dog. His mother's response has stayed with me ever since. She simply replied: "They love her." Thus ended my first exposure to the insanity of Sexual Love.

Years later, whenever I would see a couple of human males fighting over some young lady, I would think back to that day and conclude we really aren't much different from dogs. I have seen many a human male tremble with excitement (just as those dogs did) whenever they were close to an especially sensual woman. And yes, fighting for her affection is still common.

Sex is one huge motivator in life. We pretend to be casual about it, but the rabid dog in us comes out all too often. Men, it has been estimated, think about sex every eight seconds on any given day. When sexually attracted to someone, men and women alike are quick to conclude they are *in love*.

Lest you think it is only men who are obsessed, stop and peruse the current women's magazines. Sex is plastered all over the covers. You will find articles like, "Seven Ways to Make Sure Your Man Is Sexually Satisfied," "Six Positions that Guarantee the Greatest Pleasure," and "Five Facts Men Wish Women Knew about Male Bodies." Men's magazines follow the same basic theme but aren't as bashful in their approach.

It is important to note that our prurient inclinations, in combination with our desire for love, sell those magazines.

Two of the most common articles that appear regularly ask: "Is Sex Love?" or "Do Love and Sex Always Go Hand in Hand?"

I frequently rifle through these articles at the checkout stand, and am not overly surprised to read that while love and sex aren't exactly the same, it is difficult to maintain the perfect romantic relationship if sex isn't a large part of one's love.

It would seem logical to agree with these views of love; and I do. In fact, if one combines the pleasures of Sexual Love with those of Attachment Love, the resulting relationship can be absolutely fantastic. Since love is directly related to pleasure, if you can't find love between two people under those circumstances, it probably doesn't exist. Still, unless some form of Intellectual Love is present in a relationship, the romance may be fleeting—pleasantly fleeting, perhaps, but fleeting nonetheless.

Attraction as Love

For about the millionth time, someone in one of my seminars asked if I believed in love at first sight. My answer has always been an emphatic yes. So much of love and the process of falling in love is sexual in nature. Being highly attracted to someone is simply nature's way of encouraging the initial reproductive process. The hormones that rush through our bodies when we are near someone attractive are some of the most exciting in life. That may appear to be rather shallow, but it doesn't change the fact we are designed this way. The truth is, we are attracted to nicely proportioned people because, generally, they are mentally and physically healthier, making them more desirable.

This is an important point.

> If one combines the pleasures of Sexual Love with those of Attachment Love, the resulting relationships can be absolutely fantastic.

Attraction deals directly with the propagation of the species, making it extremely critical in determining the future health and look of mankind. While people are often made to feel guilty and shallow for preferring to be around attractive individuals, this is as it should be. Although I have no direct evidence for this, I am convinced scientists could undoubtedly locate an exact area of the brain in each of us that "lights up" whenever we are around an attractive person. The hormones being released feel good to us just as much as when we view a beautiful sunset.

Before proceeding, I need to make one more comment about the power of attraction. Have you ever noticed how cute and adorable babies are? Not only infants, but also puppies, kittens, and most other domesticated animals. My question is: If they weren't so cute, would they have survived around mankind?

Love and the Power of Hormones

In my imagination, I picture you, the reader, sitting in your easy chair while reading this book. You glance at your watch and realize that time has flown by and you have missed your normally scheduled dinnertime. Using the stern willpower of a true intellectual, you determine to finish the next chapter before you start to fix dinner. But, alas, hunger pains have magically begun to make their presence known, your willpower fades, and you find yourself with your nose in the refrigerator.

The questions are: How did your body succeed in getting you to open the refrigerator? What mechanism prompted you to stop reading and to seek food instead? How did the hunger pains develop? What are they and why is it so hard to ignore them?

When my oldest son was five, he and I went to a movie together. I bought him a bag of licorice, which he began to eat at a rapid pace. Several times I warned him not to eat too much since he would undoubtedly get a tummy ache. I was about to take the bag away from him when he tugged at my shirtsleeve and handed me the candy. He then directed me thusly: "Daddy, if my hand wants another piece, don't give any to it." I still laugh about that today because he had stated what we all sometimes feel to be true. Our bodies have minds of their own.

This is a great example of how, at times, our intellect has only limited control over our behavior. Numerous internal biochemical changes transfer personal control from our intellect to our emotions, needs, and desires. This transfer of control explains much irrational behavior—especially behavior connected to the feelings of love.

Finding answers to these dilemmas is finally the stuff of science. For instance, we now know those obnoxious hunger pains are caused by biochemical reactions that affect an exact area of the brain. If an MRI scan were done on someone and that part of the brain was found to be active, the technician could tell the person was hungry. Similarly, if the technician were to stimulate that area of the brain with a small electrical current, the patient would feel hunger pains.

We also know that feelings of love are located in an exact area of the brain known as the *caudate nucleus*. These conclusions were arrived at by Dr. Helen Fisher, a prominent anthropologist at Rutgers University, in an ingenious series of experiments on volunteers who stated they were passionately in love. Whenever her subjects thought about the person they were in love with, the caudate nucleus lit up.

These types of experiments have been performed for decades, resulting in the general conclusion that *all sensations, perceptions, feelings, emotions, desires, etc., are simply brain functions—which implies that one can't have an opinion, belief, desire, or feeling without first having a brain.*

I make this statement to make it clear that love and other abstract concepts like caring, having affection for, or even hate, are best explained biochemically and behaviorally rather than abstractly. Mystical or magical love is too difficult to understand and each person using the word is free to define it personally—resulting in misunderstanding and miscommunication with others.

When I was developing many of the ideas contained in this book years ago, there was not much support from biologists, neurologists, or any other medical scientists. Biologists, for example, didn't seem to care about the nature of love since it appeared to be the stuff of psychology, sociology, and religion. Scientifically based research was limited. Love was simply lumped in with the positive emotions and left at that.

Since that time, however, science has begun to make connections between feelings of love and various hormonal activities. It appears that, as Dr. Fisher pointed out, feelings of love may be created in a manner similar to those of hunger, thirst, and other needs. My more social and less anatomically descriptive conclusion is that *even feelings of love are absolutely predictable to some degree.*

One of the discoveries we are all familiar with involves the role of testosterone in human sexual behavior. Testosterone is the principle hormone in motivating humans to desire sexual contact. Its presence or absence can determine the level of sexual activity in both men and women. A sex addict may have testosterone aplenty while someone seldom sexually active may suffer from a severe absence of the hormone.

Testosterone is undoubtedly responsible for the initiation of most romantic relationships. The feelings connected to its presence in the bloodstream have been portrayed in several descriptive ways: lustful, passionate, licentious, coveting, craving, hungry for, desirous of, etc. Without testosterone, Sexual Love wouldn't be the superstar it is. In almost all societies, ours included, the sexual rush of testosterone is referred to as love and it is with a great deal of passion and fervor that we tell our lovers we love them.

Finally, because both love and sex are so complicated, I think it is important to realize there are also several classes of sexual urges motivating people toward intercourse. Testosterone-driven sex is not always responsible for normal everyday sex. People often have sex simply because it feels good. Rarely do we tremble with excitement in anticipation of the glorious event. That detail can help explain much of the miscommunication around sex between long-term lovers.

This first type of love is rather self-explanatory so I won't dwell on it any longer. Sexual Love accounts for one of the main reasons we use the phrase "I love you," and it certainly fits my definition of love as pleasure.

Harry: *You realize, of course, that we could never be friends.*
Sally: *Why not?*
Harry: *What I'm saying is—and this is not a come-on in any way, shape or form—is that men and women can't be friends because the sex part always gets in the way.*
Sally: *That's not true. I have a number of men friends and there is no sex involved.*
Harry: *No, you don't.*
Sally: *Yes, I do.*
Harry: *No, you don't.*
Sally: *Yes, I do.*
Harry: *You only think you do.*
Sally: *You say I'm having sex with these men without my knowledge?*
Harry: *No, what I'm saying is they all want to have sex with you.*
Sally: *They do not.*
Harry: *Do too.*
Sally: *They do not.*
Harry: *Do too.*
Sally: *How do you know?*
Harry: *Because no man can be friends with a woman that he finds attractive. He always wants to have sex with her.*
Sally: *So, you're saying that a man can be friends with a woman he finds unattractive?*
Harry: *No. You pretty much want to nail 'em too.*
Sally: *What if they don't want to have sex with you?*
Harry: *Doesn't matter, because the sex thing is already out there so the friendship is ultimately doomed and that's the end of the story.*
Sally: *Well, I guess we're not going to be friends then.*
Harry: *I guess not.*
Sally: *That's too bad. You're the only person I know in New York.*
From the movie: *When Harry Met Sally*

Chapter 5

Attachment Love:
The Most Powerful Love

"Love is a strange bewilderment which overtakes one person on account of another person."

~ James Thurber, Is Sex Necessary?

SCIENTISTS HAVE ISOLATED SEVERAL HORMONES THAT CAUSE pleasurable feelings in people during positive sexual and nonsexual social contact with other humans. Several of the more interesting are oxytocin, vasopressin, dopamine and serotonin. These hormones, produced in the brain and released into the body during "loving times" in our lives, seem to contain the keys as to why we feel so fantastic when we are near the people we love. For our purposes, all you need to know is that *the primitive area of the brain produces and appropriately directs glands to release various hormones and chemicals in order to promote life-giving behavior.* Whether referring to hunger pains, sexual arousal, creepy feelings about snakes, or pleasurable feelings encouraging social bonding, the end goal remains the same—survival.

Looking at the diagram on page 29, you will see that Attachment Love follows the path of Survival of the Species. Thus, even on an individual level, we are designed to be social beings for purposes of survival. (As a species, humans aren't physically impressive—we aren't that fast or large compared with other animals. It would appear our survival depends on our intelligence and *strength in numbers*.)

Following this logic would lead us to conclude that *the brain developed a reward system whereby we are made to feel good whenever we perform critical survival tasks with or for others in our group*. This reward system developed simply into the production and release of numerous hormones at precisely the moment we do something essentially unselfish. These wonderful feelings occur especially in intimate relationships, such as those with spouses, children, and siblings but they also occur whenever we help strangers in need.

As an example, it has been determined that as soon as a new mother begins nursing her baby, oxytocin is released into her bloodstream establishing a close bond between her and the infant. Without developing this beneficial bond, the child's ability to survive is challenged.

Similarly, sexual intercourse between lovers also causes the release of several of the attachment hormones. In fact, oxytocin has been referred to as the "cuddle hormone" by a number of researchers. When men and women alike describe the intimate cuddling that occurs after sex as being some of the best moments in life, they are describing the feelings created by oxytocin and other hormones. *They also express feelings of profound love during those times.*

For a moment, think about this from the other perspective. The opposing side of the graph, Survival of the Individual, naturally implies egocentric selfish behavior. One might refer to feelings (and the hormonal activity) on that side as being "I" instead of "you" behavior. But, if we only worried about ourselves as individuals, Homo sapiens would not be around today. Thus "you" oriented hormones are necessary for the survival of mankind and they help one feel Attachment Love. These "you" oriented hormones and the feelings they create are necessary for attachment love.

The Pleasures of Love Exposed

Could it be then, that much of loving behavior is simply biochemical? When people become attached to someone, is it possible the relationship is substantially motivated by the good feelings caused by hormones? Could we, therefore, even cause a selfish person to become unselfish by simply injecting him with a particular hormone? In reverse, is it possible that people who don't *care* about others are merely lacking the ability to produce a certain hormone and might then be suffering from a malfunction in some area of the brain? Or is it the other way around? Are people who care too much merely responding to an over supply of some chemical?

If a lover receives a shot of a pleasurable hormone when he gives his beloved a gift, is this a loving act or is he merely being selfish? Was he selfishly seeking to experience feelings of joy himself or was his aim to make her feel good? And when they both feel good, have they "found" love?

How about this question: If two people in love stop having sex together, do the attachment hormones begin to disappear? Apparently they do, which might explain why Attachment Love all too often slowly begins to fade after the initial passionate sexual phase of a relationship. From a practical perspective then, is there anything that can be done to prevent the faded passion? Could *insisting* on frequent sex with a loved one actually enhance the quality of the entire relationship, even in the absence of long-lost lust? Could doing so release oxytocin and other hormones, thus holding the relationship together for affectionate rather than sexual reasons?

> Could it be then, that much of loving behavior is simply biochemical?

The questions are numerous. Let's mull over these ideas and look at some of the results of these hormonal releases. Without being too particular about which hormone, chemical reaction, or even which part of the brain is being affected to cause positive feelings, let's look at a few of the times when people *feel* attachment love.

Love Feelings Controlled

Feelings associated with love are caused by the release of hormones. With this knowledge, I can essentially trick my body into releasing hormones that create great feelings. You might say I have learned to seek pleasant feelings in a somewhat manipulative fashion. Since these feelings come from the Survival of the Species side of the outline, it only makes sense that I need to involve other people if I want to experience those pleasures. Following is something I wrote several years ago that explains how this works.

> " . . . my eight-year-old son interrupted my writing by craftily maneuvering himself onto my lap. I had been concentrating very hard while the cursor blinked on the screen . . . I was so totally blank and uninspired that I didn't really mind that he was interrupting me.
>
> As usual, my son wanted to wrestle and be tickled. Evidently, I needed to do the same because I immediately proceeded to play with him. I tickled, kissed, hugged, and then hugged, tickled and kissed him for fifteen minutes. For a while afterwards, he sat silently on my lap while I hugged him tightly, rubbed his back, and told him how much his daddy loved him. The pleasure I received from him was incredible. I never wanted to let him go. It was as if I were soaking up love from his sweet touches."

Just reading this passage stirs up intense feelings of love for my son. I can feel the hormones doing their job. My inclination, even as I type, is to find him and hug him again and again. What a deal! I please him and he pleases me. You can't beat that.

Can you now begin to sense how people are biologically designed? What a perfect design this is too. *Attachment hormones create all of those wonderful feelings.* They keep us coming back for more, time after time, which, it seems, is exactly what we need if we are to survive happily.

The Power of Touch

When you meet someone you are mutually attracted to, it requires only a small step before expressions of love become predictable. Soon after a relationship begins, the hormones really get going and the "I love you's" proliferate.

The production and release of many of these hormones is directly caused by tactile behavior between people—even nonsexual forms of touching between friends and relatives. Touching others and being touched by them creates pleasures not available in any other fashion. A good hug goes a long way toward making someone feel worthwhile.

> Touching others and being touched by them creates pleasures not available in any other fashion.

Interestingly, you can't cause most of the pleasure hormones to be released in your own body without someone else being involved. In other words, you can't experience the same release of pleasing hormones by touching yourself as when being touched by others. In this sense alone, it can be said we need other people. There is an immense difference between rubbing your own feet and in having them rubbed by someone else. The pleasure is entirely different. This release of pleasurable hormones reinforces attachment love.

Marasmus

Years ago, orphanages were widespread throughout this country and they were filled with children. During the Depression, prior to the existence of effective forms of birth control, parents often had few other choices but to leave their children in orphanages.

You might not think the age of a child makes any difference to an orphanage, but it does. A baby requires more direct care than an older child. Consequently, because of time constraints, caretakers were prone to prop a baby's bottle up against a pillow.

As a result of this lack of one-on-one attention and physical touch, there was a high mortality rate among babies.

Before they died, the infants seemed to waste away. Ultimately, this condition was given the name "marasmus." The babies' health went slowly downhill—until they died. For years, no one could figure out why these children were dying. It seemed to everyone that their physical needs were being met and they were being well cared for generally, yet the deaths were still occurring.

One of the conclusions finally reached was that the babies lacked a mother's love. If there is anything more powerful than love, it's *mother's* love. But what exactly is mother's love?

The debate eventually focused on the *actions* a mother performs when she cares for her baby. The conclusion was that mothering involves cuddling, kissing, hugging, and caressing. After the introduction of this type of contact (mothering) into orphanages, the mortality rate dropped significantly.

We can now draw a conclusion about the relationship between touch and love. Man's need for tactile stimulation is strong. Consider how my son sought my attention by interrupting my writing, and how joyfully I exchanged cuddles and back-scratches with him. Consider how critical touch is to babies; and finally, consider how falling in love is so closely tied to making love. The need in humans to touch and to be touched can't be overemphasized. Even kissing can be directly tied to feelings of happiness, i.e., people who are kissing others express more satisfaction with life in general. Unfortunately, in my opinion, few people are being touched or kissed enough and our desire to be touched is almost desperate.

Touching reinforces Attachment Love. With that conclusion, we can now feel love in the true sense of the word. Love is now more real than before—more treasured than ever. No love relationship is worth having without the presence of touch. Love is no longer simply a vague pleasure; it is precisely connected to the pleasure of touching.

Good friends always touch! Lovers always touch! Parents always touch their children! Even strangers will touch in times of crises. The more frequently and earnestly two people touch each other, the more likely it is they will have a great relationship.

Once we find someone willing to exchange touching behavior with us, even if a large percentage of the touching is nonsexual, the rush of pleasure can overtake us and lead to a strong *affection* for that individual. And, when the touching becomes sexual, the intensity of the pleasure is magnified. Our need to touch others is critical to our happiness and contentment. By nature our survival depends on touching and it plays a large role in Attachment Love.

In his book *Touching: The Human Significance of the Skin*, Ashley Montagu said it beautifully: "By being stroked, and caressed, and carried, and cuddled, and cooed to, by being loved, (a child) learns to stroke and caress and cuddle, and coo to and love others."

The Big A's

It took me a while to notice there are three words we use to discuss close personal relationships that all begin with the letter "A". They are attachment, attraction, and affection. In a good relationship, all three would be present in abundance. Whether referring to a parent/child, boyfriend/girlfriend, husband/wife or friend/friend relationship, there should be attachment, attraction, and affection. And, it goes without saying: they are all products of feelings created by hormones.

I recently observed a young mother in a restaurant taking care of her six-month-old baby. She must have kissed him on the cheek fifty times. I could sense how intensely she loved him. It gushed out of her. I also recognized how the big A's fit into their relationship. Obviously the baby was thriving because there was little doubt about her attraction, affection, and attachment for her child. It was a truly beautiful thing to watch.

The attachment hormones often override the sex hormones in their level of importance in a relationship. One's affection for another can hold steady, even under trying circumstances. This is beautifully described in the following brief story written by

Richard Selzer, MD in his book, *Mortal Lessons: Notes in the Art of Surgery*, New York: Simon & Schuster, 1976, pgs 45-46.

> "I stand by the bed where a young woman lies, her face postoperative, her mouth twisted in palsy, clownish. A tiny twig of the facial nerve, the one to the muscles of her mouth, has been severed. She will be thus from now on. The surgeon had followed with religious fervor the curve of her flesh; I promise you that. Nevertheless, to remove the tumor in her cheek, I had to cut the little nerve.
>
> Her young husband is in the room. He stands on the opposite side of the bed, and together they seem to dwell in the evening lamplight, isolated from me, private. Who are they, I ask myself, he and this wry-mouth I have made, who gaze at and touch each other so generously, greedily? The young woman speaks.
>
> "Will my mouth always be like this?" she asks.
>
> "Yes," I say, "it will. It is because the nerve was cut."
>
> She nods, and is silent. But the young man smiles.
>
> "I like it," he says. "It is kind of cute."
>
> All at once I know who he is. I understand, and I lower my gaze. One is not bold in an encounter with a god. Unmindful, he bends to kiss her crooked mouth, and I, so close I can see how he twists his own lips to accommodate to hers, to show her that their kiss still works. I remember that the gods appeared in ancient Greece as mortals, and I hold my breath and let the wonder in."

In Love

Earlier we discussed an approach to love as it relates to the pleasures of life. This section on Attachment Love concludes that pleasurable feelings caused by hormones encourage us to say "I love you" to others. However, the question arises as to whether or not we love everyone who pleases us. Most generally, we do *not*.

The English language is full of insidious little confusions that make things difficult to understand, and the way we use the word *love* is no exception. Consider this: while you were reading the above paragraph, it would have been normal for you to disagree with the comment that we don't generally love those who please us. However, by adding one small word, the meaning can be changed and made more acceptable. If the sentence read: "The question arises as to whether or not we are *in* love with the people who please us," fewer people would object when the final sentence read: "Most generally we are not *in love* with them."

The point to be made here helps explain some of the confusion about the concept of love. Loving someone and being in love with that individual are two entirely different ideas. It is culturally acceptable to love many things, from one's friends to apple pie, but we reserve being *in love* for more definite circumstances.

One might easily say that he loves his dog, but he would be considered a bit strange if he were to say that he was in love with his dog. The same applies to human relationships. A man's daughter may love him, and that is expected, but it would not be socially acceptable for her to be in love with him.

We can all feel this to be true; yet we may not know why it is true. The phrase *in love* is, at times, objectionable for two reasons. In the first place, *in love* usually implies a sexual relationship, making it unacceptable in a father-daughter relationship because of the incestuous connotation. In this context, neither the father nor daughter, nor anyone else for that matter, may use the phrase—unless it is used to describe one's relationship with a socially acceptable sex partner.

Should a man state that he is in love with another man, there are homosexual implications. Peculiarly, if a man were to state he was in love with a woman, an acceptable sex partner, the sexual implication isn't as strong. The suggestion that the couple might be having a sexual relationship exists, but the implication switches and begins to suggest more of an emotional involvement between the two.

This concept of Emotional Love is the second reason why one finds objection to the indiscriminate use of the phrase *in love*. It doesn't sound appropriate to say that you are emotionally involved with your dog, or your father, or your automobile, or anything else that you may perfectly well say you love.

Look again at the Survival diagram on page 29. From this discussion it can be concluded that there is a barrier between Sexual Love and Attachment Love. Attachment Love involves many sorts of pleasurable feelings caused by contact with others. However those pleasures usually cannot become sexual. Societal prescriptions prevent such from happening.

Summary

According to scientists, there are at least a thousand hormones being produced and released inside our bodies whose job it is to prompt us to perform survival-oriented behavior. Based on the Survival diagram, these hormones would logically belong to two separate classes: some involved with our relationships with other people and the remainder involved with our own survival.

The presence of some of the thousand hormones is pleasurable, valued, and sought after; while others (which we haven't discussed yet) are unpleasant and, therefore, strenuously avoided. Interestingly, I think most of the pleasurable hormones are found on the Survival of the Species side. The pain-stimulating hormones prompt us to survive as individuals (every man for himself) by forcing us to avoid problems in the first place. Hormones that cause hunger pains are good examples of this.

Twenty some years ago, a friend of mine was working on an interesting hypothesis that maintained that people mostly do things in order to *avoid* pain—pleasure-seeking traits were secondary. Thus, we eat to avoid hunger pains and drink to avoid thirst. From this viewpoint, hormones take on an even greater role. Without the motivating influences of hormones, we would not even eat properly.

I am inclined to agree with my friend regarding survival of the individual, but not about species survival. I doubt many people would do much for others without feeling good in the process. The prominence of hateful, mean-spirited, inconsiderate, and unkind behavior throughout civilization proves my point. Without good feelings being available, more of us would live only for personal gain. As it stands, most people appear to live life while operating on the survival of the individual side of the outline.

Love and the Aging Process

Attachment Love can best explain one of my favorite Shakespearean sonnets, and the phenomenon it describes: "Let me not to the marriage of true minds admit impediments: Love is not love which alters when it alteration finds...Love's not time's fool though rosy lips and cheeks within his bending sickles compass come; Love alters not with his brief hours and weeks, but bears it out even to the edge of doom." (Sonnet CXVI)

How is it, if we are generally drawn to the more beautiful things in nature, that a loved one, in spite of suffering from the ravages of time, can still remain beautiful? When others look, they see an old person. When a loved one looks, he sees a beautiful old person. Attachment Love and the magical hormones therein have done their job well.

I always say a girl must get married for love—and keep on getting married until she finds it.
Zsa Zsa Gabor

CHAPTER 6

Intellectual Love:
Love With a Purpose

"The more things two people have in common, the more likely it is they will have a successful relationship."
~ Dr Laura Schlessinger

THUS FAR WE HAVE DEALT WITH THE SURVIVAL OF THE SPECIES; THE next several chapters will discuss the Survival of the Individual, which dictates most human behavior connected with basic survival tasks like eating, getting an education, making a living, and avoiding all things dangerous. Love, or rather the practical selfish side of love, can also be understood from this perspective.

There is no significant difference between any of the four types of love; they are each designed to enhance the survival of the individual in love—not the person who is loved.

While one can claim to be lovingly altruistic toward another, the truth is people love from a completely selfish platform. Even the apparently unselfish forms of Attachment Love are selfish at the core. Consequently, to enhance the original outline, let's insert two new phrases. On the Survival of the Species side, the phrase "apparently unselfish" will be added; and on the other side, the phrase "obviously selfish" will be added. The additions

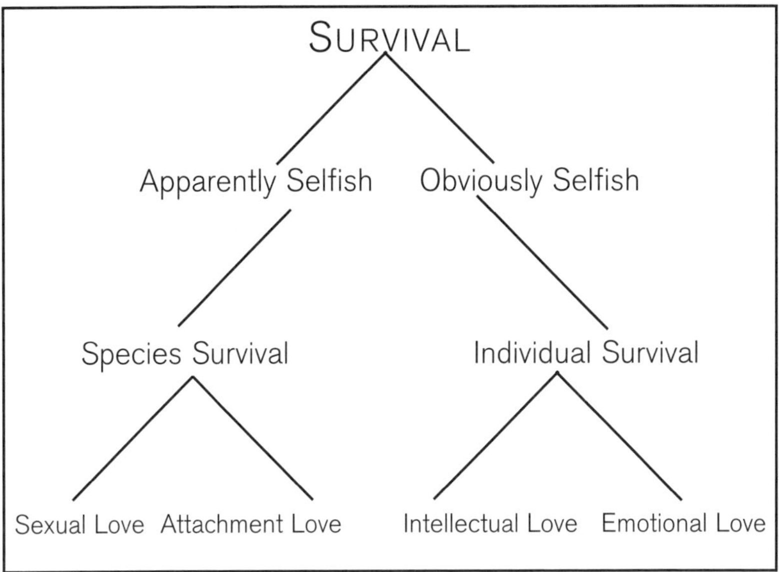

are made as a reminder that no matter how one wants to tease oneself, all behavior is still a product of survival.

When I exchanged loving touches with my son, I did so because it felt wonderful to *me*. Both of us behaved selfishly—but both also profited! If all exchanges of love were designed thusly, the world would be an amazing place. Let's take a look at the various aspects of Intellectual Love.

Absolute Practicality

Sometimes the wondrous feelings associated with falling in and being in love are secondary to the more necessary parts of life, like eating and keeping a roof over one's head. Practicality often dictates that we make decisions about our future with a much less romantic eye than we might otherwise choose. Marrying the wrong person because of passion, lust, or other feelings can lead to years of unhappiness.

Whether we like to admit it or not, sometimes it is best to seek relationships that will lead to a comfortable, uncomplicated, secure life with someone similar in thought, beliefs, interests, and attitudes.

> Could it be that establishing a quality relationship is more a function of intelligence rather than feelings?

Maybe the sincerely nice person will make a better marriage partner than the sexy hunk. Maybe the hard-working college student with definite goals will make a better marriage partner than the free-spirited adventurer. Maybe others around you are correct when they say your current choice is not a good match for you.

Could it be that establishing a quality relationship is more a function of intelligence rather than feelings? Are the sweethearts among us better marriage choices than the more exciting but perhaps selfish souls? Yes, indeed! Maybe love should be as practical as possible (which is why I have referred to this section as Intellectual Love).

The Truth about Love

In the first chapter I postulated that love is directly related to the amount of pleasure one receives from the love object. The focus was on the word *pleasure*. We love that which pleases us. It's that simple. Things pleasurable to us are valued because they somehow enhance our survival.

Is it possible for this pleasure-seeking perspective of love to be altruistic or selfless in any way? Could we ever do things for those we love without some sort of personal pleasure being connected?

Consider the phrase "I love you." Which of the two pronouns is the most important? Classically, "you" is the most important for various *selfless* reasons. *You* are wonderful, fantastic, sexy, considerate, kind, thoughtful, funny, etc. I can't live without *you*. I love *you* because *you're you*. I need *you*.

Where is the truth? Would, could, or should someone ever claim to love another unless that other person were somehow satisfying some *selfish* need? Isn't the pronoun "I" more important because it is closer to the truth?

"I love you" is, thus, more easily interpreted to mean, "You please me." This simple approach is less confusing and seems like the perfect description of love.

Go back to the sentence involving the "you" part of the phrase. By rewriting everything, the truth becomes more apparent. You are wonderful—because you please *me*. You are sexy and that gives *me* pleasure. You are considerate which is pleasing to *me*. You are successful, intelligent, funny, and thoughtful—all of which somehow pleases *me*.

One of my favorite quotes about love is from Robert A. Heinlein in *Strangers in a Strange Land*. He states: "Love is that condition where the happiness of another is essential to your own." As far as I'm concerned, his description is about as selfless as love will ever be. It describes the need in all of us to do things to please those we love because *we receive pleasure in the process*. Sharing a beautiful sunset, giving the perfect gift, saying just the right thing—these are all examples of the perfect way to enjoy the pleasures of love. Simply put—when it pleases you to please another—love has been discovered. Love can be practical, logical, and intellectual. Long-lasting love relationships usually are. Think about it.

I Like You

The most powerful phrase one can ever hope to hear in a relationship and the words everyone prays they will hear are: "I love you." It is sadly ironic that one might be much better off if a lover were to say instead: "I like you." Love has too much folklore and confusion surrounding it—too many ambiguities. "I like you" is more desirable and much less confusing. One of the reasons I maintain this attitude is that people often claim to love others they don't even like. That phenomenon makes love look foolish and illogical.

So the question becomes: What makes a person likable? I have always noted that when it comes to personality types, wherein one's *behavior* is the main consideration, people range from self-centered to endearing. All of us fit somewhere in between the two extremes. From infancy, humans begin life as selfish beings; the changes occur as our parents and society mold us to be considerate of other people before pleasing ourselves. The more we succeed at pleasing others, the more likeable we become. Hence the praise: "That person is such a sweetheart!"

Of course, as with all other scales in life, this one follows the normal curve, i.e., the large majority of us fall in the middle of the scale—we have a little bit of both in our personalities. Maturity develops as we learn to control our selfish desires and put others' desires ahead of our own.

I have been monitoring the personal ads in the newspapers and on the Internet in an attempt to decide what singles are looking for in a mate. It appears people are fooling themselves. You see, most of the ads read like a sweetheart thesaurus. Everyone seems to be searching for someone who is kind, considerate, wholesome, funny, compassionate, gentle, good-natured, warm, and friendly. Yet—*no one actually dates those people*—unless they are also attractive, sexy, athletic, outdoorsy, and/or financially secure. That leaves 90 percent of us out of the game, even if we might be sweethearts.

To prove my point I interviewed the manager of a large dating service that used pictures and videos to introduce people to potential lovers. Just as I predicted, the *average* lonely soul in the company files seldom *ever* got picked out of the crowd. They paid the same for the service but got nothing in return. No one ever expressed any desire to meet them.

But, if on the rare occasions when a sexy, attractive person signed up (male or female), they were inundated with requests for dates—so many that before long they usually cancelled their memberships or put them on hold for indefinite terms.

What is interesting about that phenomenon is that even the people *not being chosen* by others refuse to pick those who are much like themselves. It's like they decide that even if others find them to be undesirable, they aren't about to lower their own standards in order to meet someone who isn't *attractive* to them.

Mother Nature and hormones are busy frustrating us again. I would like to lay most of the blame on the men in the group since we admittedly seek sexy, attractive women to date, but the average man seldom gets contacted either.

So, what people say and what people do is quite different when it comes to love. For Intellectual Love to succeed, we need to look beyond the package and realize that a sweetheart is going to give us a better relationship than someone who looks good but acts otherwise.

If you want to read about love and marriage, you've got to buy two separate books.
> Alan King

CHAPTER 7

Emotional Love:
Insane With Love

"No word is used with more meanings than this term (love), most of the meanings being dishonest in that they cover up the real underlying motives in the relationship."

~ Rollo May

I DISAGREE WITH MUCH THAT HAS ALREADY BEEN WRITTEN ABOUT love. Not about the pleasures of love, but rather about the pain associated with it. I have hinted at this disagreement several times, but will now disclose why I see love differently.

I reserve the use of the word *love* to express feelings connected with pleasure. Sexual, Attachment, and Intellectual Love fit this usage. However—the entire world seems to believe love is an emotion—while I do not. If one refers to the pleasures connected with love as being some form of *positive* emotion, I would readily agree; but the emotion-called-love is generally synonymous with heartbreak—a negative feeling.

Many declarations of love are made because of the negative emotions created by problems within a relationship. I don't know how many songs have been written about love wherein love is said to hurt. I even discussed this aspect in Chapter 1, when I referred to my high-school romance and the pain I went through after our breakup. At the time, I believed the intensity of my pain proved my love. Those conclusions were normal and acceptable. The general inclination in all of us is to refer to the resultant heartbreak as being proof of Emotional Love.

Since then, I have switched my beliefs to the point where I now maintain that the pain associated with love is only indirectly connected with love. One can believe himself to be in love with someone, even when the relationship is horrible and no pleasure is evident.

To distinguish my philosophy from the rest of the world, I have coined the phrase "emotion–called-love." It is neither accurate nor appropriate to refer to love as being an emotion; so to make this concept clear, I will examine a few imaginary relationships and predict the emotional process referred to as falling in love.

I watched a movie the other day that included a perfectly appropriate scene for this discussion. The handsome hero is dating a luscious woman. After only a few dates, he looks deeply into her eyes and confesses: "I think I am falling in love with you. I can't imagine living the rest of my life without you." It was a very romantic scene, but my desire to disclose his motives ruined it for me. I mean, really! What is he telling her? If this were his way of seducing her, then we would have to conclude his testosterone was ablaze and he was therefore referring to Sexual Love. If he was referring to Attachment Love, he might be expressing a sincere fondness for her because she was so cute, sweet, and fun to be with. From an Intellectual Love standpoint, he could be referring to her popularity in town or her wealth.

I can identify with these expressions of love; though it seems as if his expression of potential love was more indicative of an emotional connection when he claimed not being able to live without her. Could he have become that attached to her so quickly? This implies a needy emotional connection; an emotional upheaval in her absence. Did he really mean he needed her that much so soon in the relationship? How is this possible? Should she approach this relationship with caution? What is the truth?

Let's search for the truth. Let's look at this process of falling in love (emotionally) and see if we can determine how it occurs. By doing so, perhaps we can clear up much of the confusion associated with falling in love.

Falling In Love

Falling in love is a process whereby we begin to need another person more and more until we ultimately reach a point where we need that person *desperately*. This process has gone on since the beginning of civilization. It is systematic, precise, and *predictable*; yet most people are unaware of exactly how it occurs.

By observing people's behavior, I have developed a seven-step formula that describes how people emotionally fall in love. The steps to the formula, which we will go through in the next chapter, are merely observations of an everyday process we all regularly witness.

The formula clarifies the process of falling in love and can be used like a love potion of sorts. Yet, even though the process can be outlined, mapped out, and followed, the end result is no different than if you were to fall in love without being aware of the formula. In truth, falling in love with someone by accident is no better than falling in love on purpose. In fact, from a logical standpoint, it is better if people know what they are doing while they are falling in love.

The knowledge of what is happening as a relationship develops doesn't lessen the pleasure and can actually serve to make the relationship more pleasurable since it can prevent problems that might develop. There is no human being more pitiful to behold than one whose heart has been broken and who doesn't understand what happened or even how it happened. The emotional devastation one feels during times of heartbreak is so severe that if a love potion could actually be bottled (like in fairy tales), the bottle would have to carry a warning from the surgeon general. Maybe even the classic skull and crossbones would be required on the label, along with the warning: "The contents of this bottle could be hazardous to your emotional health."

I have witnessed people begin a relationship that seemed doomed from the start. I have been tempted to approach them and plead with them and warn them that someone is going to be hurt, and then beg them to listen to me while I tell them how and why this will occur and what they can do to prevent disaster from striking. (That is exactly what this book is attempting to accomplish.)

So, before I discuss how to fall in love, I need to clarify that, although there may be a formula for falling in love, it is not my intention to suggest you necessarily do so. One risks a great deal in any relationship. Sometimes the risk is worth it; sometimes it is not. If you fall in love with the wrong person you might suffer severely, both emotionally and physically.

Unfortunately, there are many bad people on this earth. Getting involved with one of them because you are lonely or they are good-looking or rich or whatever is not the wisest thing to do. This advice may seem obvious, but what is not so obvious is that falling in love with a kind, considerate, and generally nice person can be nearly as emotionally devastating. Being intimately involved with someone with different views or beliefs about life, especially over long periods of time, can be difficult. It's undoubtedly wiser to look for someone with similar views and then fall in love.

Remember this: I do want you to fall in love and to be loved in return. There is nothing more wonderful in life than doing so. I simply want to educate you on the process, giving you more control and better relationships.

When my wife has sex with me there's always a reason. One night she used me to time an egg.
Rodney Dangerfield

CHAPTER 8

A Formula for Emotional Love: Love by the Numbers

*"What are the fields or flow'rs, or all I see? Ah!
Tasteless all, if not enjoy'd with thee."*
~ Thomas Parnell, Health, An Eclogue

IN THIS CHAPTER, I WILL SHOW YOU HOW TO CATCH YOURSELF a lover. While this sounds cold-hearted, people have been doing this for years; I'm merely putting in black and white what is actually occurring. Even sweet old grandmothers use phrases like "catch your man" or "trap yourself a husband" when giving advice to their granddaughters. The only difference between the grandmothers' methods and those described in this chapter is one of awareness of what causes the emotion–called-love to occur.

Once I developed the seven-step formula for falling in love, I had fun sharing it with my high school and college students. Their enthusiasm was heartwarming. However, when deciding how to present the formula in this book, I face a peculiar dilemma.

It turns out that putting the formula on paper and letting strangers read it doesn't get the same positive reactions as from my students. In fact, some readers view the formula as being manipulative and somewhat creepy. They see it as a plot against an unsuspecting victim. I can't tell you how many people have given me the silent treatment after reading the formula.

I seriously considered rearranging the formula. In its current form, it is set up to show readers how to get someone to fall in love with them, which is why it seems so manipulative. I could have presented the information differently, like a case study on how people fall in love; but I have chosen to leave it in this form to demonstrate how shallow and predictable the emotion-called-love can be.

The idea behind the following formula is to give you power over your love life. Once this formula for falling in love is exposed, the emotion-called-love will have no power over you. After all, if the emotion can be created by design—-should you rely on it to make life's major decisions?

So, I present the formula with the admonition that using it for selfish reasons is reprehensible. Having said that, let's begin.

Step One: Establish Relationship Goals

When a man does not know what harbor he is making for, no wind is the right wind.

SENECA, Epistulae ad Lucilium

Step one involves self-analysis. The purpose of this step is to firmly establish your goals in reference to a relationship. While most people wouldn't mind falling in love and having someone fall in love with them, you may not be ready for a total commitment involving, for example, marriage. You might simply be looking for companionship or a casual sexual relationship.

While this step may not appear to be too important in the formula, it is one of the most important. Unless goals are established in all areas of life, it is too easy to allow the world to control your life for you. Purposeful, goal-directed behavior makes you more likely to succeed in your endeavors. In regard to love, the need to have firmly established goals is doubly important because you are influencing another person's life. From this perspective, that person's goals should also be considered before embarking on your journey leading to love.

One of the more interesting conversations I ever had was with a gentleman who would be considered by most women to be a hunk. He told me that very early in life, he realized girls fell in love with him rather easily. At first it was flattering and exciting. As time went by, though, it became frustrating. He grew cynical about love, to say the least. As a result, he rarely dated. Why?

Well, he figured out that if he dated a woman more than four or five times, she would invariably think she was in love. Thus, unless he was extremely interested in the lady, he wasn't going to lead her on. It was too hard to break off the relationships if he did otherwise. Too many tears! Too much emotion! Too many scenes! It was simpler to prevent a relationship from developing in the first place.

I found his approach to be honorable. Maybe more people should adopt his style.

You sleep with a guy once and before you know it, he wants to take you to dinner.

Myers Yori

Step Two: Meeting Someone

No matter what, no matter when, no matter who; any man has a chance to sweep any woman off her feet. He just needs the right broom. Alex "Hitch" Hitchens

From the movie: *Hitch*

Before you can fall in love, several criteria must be satisfied. First, you must meet the person; you can fall in love only with someone you know exists. This person does not necessarily have to know you, but you, at least in some way, have to know her. For example, it is theoretically possible that a man could fall in love with a movie star because he sees her on the screen, thinks about her often, and even dreams about her at night. However, she is not going to fall in love with him because she doesn't know him.

People have fallen in love with strangers when the only interaction between them was walking past each other every day at work or school. This distant love is highly unsatisfying since it is one-sided. Poets refer to this as "unrequited love."

This step of the formula is effective in pointing out that in order to fall in love with someone, you have to be available to meet that person in the first place. People who are isolated at home and who never socialize with others can't expect to find someone to fall in love with them. Therefore, if you desire to fall in love, you must do whatever is necessary in order to meet other people. I'll comment more on this later, but in the meantime, remember that people must seek love, for love won't seek them.

Love and eggs should be fresh to be enjoyed.
Russian Proverb

Step Three: Feeling and Creating an Attraction

Kindness is worth more than beauty.
Jean D'Arras, *Melusine*

The next step to falling in love with someone is controlled by the rule of attraction. Simply stated, the rule of attraction points out that you fall in love only with someone who is attractive to you in some way. And the more attracted you are to someone, the more likely you are to fall in love with her.

The more you watch for the rule of attraction in everyday life, as people around you fall in love, the more complicated it becomes. How often have you heard the question "What does she see in him?" or the statement "I'll never understand what those two see in each other"? As odd as it may seem, at times a person who is in love may not even know why he is attracted to his lover.

For the sake of clarity and organization, attraction will be divided into four basic types: physical, personality, social fame, and economic status. (There are far too many forms of attraction to deal with all of them, so I will only discuss these four to establish a base from which to work.)

Physical Attraction

People fall in love with those who are physically appealing. Even though each individual has his own tastes; there is some general agreement. For example, the classic face could be defended as the most attractive.

An encounter I once had with a young woman (I'll call her Trudy) illustrates this well. I was discussing the question of what makes a woman attractive with a group of friends when I put my vote in for the classic face. At this point, I came under attack from Trudy. Her objection was that I was a male chauvinist pig for preferring pretty women when, indeed, a plain woman could be more attractive because of her inner goodness.

Luckily for me, an artist friend took up the challenge. He sought a pencil and paper and informed Trudy that he was going to give her a new face. She could choose her own features; he would sketch them, and we could all see the result. It was obvious that Trudy was in trouble from the start, for his first witty question went something like this: "Now, Trudy, let's begin with your nose. Would you prefer one that is too small for your face, too large for your face, or one that is just right?" His Goldilocks' tone of voice made us all laugh, at which point Trudy gave up and admitted if the questioning were to continue, she would probably end up with a classic face. She even admitted that, if given a choice, she would also desire a classic figure.

The point of the story is this: if, when given a choice about our appearance, the majority of us would choose a classic face and figure (whether male or female); it stands to reason that we would also choose a person with a classic face and figure as being the most attractive. Therefore, we would also prefer to fall in love with that type of person.

The importance of a person's physical appearance cannot be overemphasized. Extremely beautiful women and handsome men never suffer from a shortage of people willing to seek their companionship and fall in love with them.

Physical attraction is *critical* in love relationships. In fact, it almost goes without saying that sex and the intense pleasures connected with it, cause all of us to fall in love. Undoubtedly, most of us at some time in our lives have been so attracted to someone we have literally trembled with excitement whenever we were close to that individual. The attraction can be so intense that we blabber incoherent sentences that make us sound foolish. Yes, indeed! Physical attraction plays a critical role in love.

Attraction to Personality

Fortunately, other things contribute to a person's attractiveness. The second type of attraction covers what is, perhaps, the most valuable and durable reason for loving someone—a great personality. Falling in love because someone has a pleasant personality is starting off on the right foot.

Ultimately, love should be logical, and there is no more logical reason for seeking another person's companionship than because she has a good personality.

In classic psychological terms, one's personality determines one's behavior. For example, an extrovert would probably be noisy and active at a party, whereas an introvert would be quiet and inactive. However, an extrovert is an extrovert because she is noisy and active, and not vice versa. Her behavior determines her personality.

The confusion here is one that is widespread throughout the field of psychology. It is always behavior that counts when discussing personality. Therefore, if you fall in love with someone because she has a good personality, what you are actually saying is that she behaves well. She treats others respectfully and kindly—and those are lovable traits.

People are lovable and should be loved because of their pleasing behavior toward you. The reverse is also true. People are not lovable and should not be loved if their behavior is aggressive. When love survives in spite of the presence of excessive aggression, it is generally a result of the emotional insecurity of the people involved.

Personality, then, is a reflection of one's actions or behavior. We are drawn to a person who has a good personality because her actions are mostly non-aggressive. In fact, her actions are pleasing. All of us feel good when we are around someone who smiles frequently, plays hard, and generally enjoys life. We are more inclined to spend time with that sort of person, and more inclined to fall in love with that person.

One may wonder why some people fall in love with those who are aggressive and vicious towards others. The answer lies in the upcoming fifth, sixth, and seventh steps that are necessary before becoming emotionally attached to someone.

It is obvious from the first two types of attraction that either one alone can be enough to cause someone to fall in love. For example, there is the beautiful woman with a rotten personality—sounds bad, but one can't deny that she would still be appealing. Or how about a homely woman with a fantastic personality (the choice of wise men according to poets)? Very attractive! And so it goes; everyone seems to have some sort of attraction for someone. The extremes were used to keep things simple. Yet, who would deny that there is a lot of appeal in being average?

Social Popularity and Fame

The next types of attraction result from the human tendency to be gregarious and seek social companionship. Until we have been over-stimulated, as is the case for many famous people, we generally like to receive attention from others. It is reasonable therefore, that being around people who are popular or famous indirectly draws attention to us.

For example, much of the appeal that celebrities seem to have may not be in their looks or personalities, but simply because of their fame. The same is true on a smaller scale: in our adolescent years the "in crowd" is sought after in the dating game. The quarterback on the football team may have nothing else to offer except his position on the team—but that is oftentimes more than enough.

Economic Status

If a person has nothing else to offer but money, sadly it is often enough. Perhaps this is why some people object to an analysis of love. The fact of the matter is that people are more appealing to others if they are rich. As Grandma used to say, "It's as easy to fall in love with a rich man as it is to fall in love with a poor man." Money can play a huge role in love. Whether we like to admit it or not, love relationships are better when money, or rather a lack of it, is not an issue. Money buys a busier and more entertaining lifestyle, making some of the other aspects of love more acceptable.

Summary

In this third step toward falling in love, we have glanced at a few of the ways people are attracted to one another. We could have saved a lot of time by reading a book of fairy tales. To answer the question of what makes someone attractive, we need only look at the heroes and heroines in fairy tales. For example, a prince is best described as a handsome gentleman who is kind and considerate, liked and admired by everyone, of great fame throughout the land—and beastly rich.

Sex without love is an empty experience, but as empty experiences go, it's one of the best.
Woody Allen

Step Four: Observing and Learning About the Person

Nothing is so difficult but that it may be found out by observing.
Terence, Heauton Timorumenos

Once your goals have been established, you can move to step four, which is observing the behavior of the desired individual. This step is necessary if you are dealing with the proverbial "tough nut to crack," i.e., the person who is sought after by many people. It also helps to avoid frustration, since you will be less likely to suffer setbacks.

The object of this step is to find out as much about the person as you can. You need to know her likes, dislikes, needs, desires, beliefs on religion and politics, and (this is important) you have to map out her schedule. You need to know what she does and with whom from the time she gets up in the morning until she goes to bed at night.

(Author's note: It is important to point out that this observation phase is not intended to mimic the mentality and tactics of a stalker. What is suggested is a casual observation of the other person's schedule. Chatting with her, asking questions of friends, or just being observant is all that is necessary.)

Generally, most people's lives are fairly consistent in that they get up in the morning at about the same time each day, eat breakfast, go to work, have lunch, return to work, go home, etc.

Even though some variation occurs from time to time, people's lives can be so routine as to be automatic.

Consequently, soon after you begin observing her, you should be able to estimate fairly accurately where she might be at any time and with whom. .

The more thoroughly you do your homework, the better off you'll be. Suppose for example, a man's subject is in the habit of bowling every Tuesday night with her friends. If he has done a thorough job of observation, he will not make the mistake of inviting her to go with him to a movie Tuesday night. This knowledge can save him the embarrassment of being turned down. Besides, it gives him invaluable information about her: she likes to bowl. Should the opportunity present itself, he might be able to arrange to bowl in a mixed-doubles league or a benefit bowl-a-thon with her as a partner.

During this step, it is important for him to figure out what things please her. Since love is really only a measurement of the pleasure being derived from the lover, he must know what she enjoys. Perhaps she loves to play a certain sport. Maybe she's a musician or a singer.

Let's take an example and explain why it is so important to know what pleases your lover. How about the dinner table? That's a perfect spot to win or lose a lover. All of us were reared in different ways when it comes to eating. Some people view eating as a basic necessity of life, while others view it as one of the greatest pleasures of life. Should a man's date be the former type, taking her to a swanky restaurant for a little elixir of the good life might make her uncomfortable; whereas if he invited her to a picnic with his friends, she might enjoy herself thoroughly.

The point is that love develops during a time of comfort or fun more readily than during a time of discomfort. Should his date be uncomfortable in his presence because of the awkward circumstance, she will be inclined to blame the discomfort on him rather than upon the circumstance. Since she "didn't have much fun," then "he isn't much fun;" which could be the end of the romance.

My sister was with two men in one night. She could hardly walk after that. Can you imagine? Two dinners?
Sarah Silverman

Step Five: Creating Time Dependency

Habit causes love.
Lucretius, DeReram Natura

In everyday life, step five begins when a couple starts dating or initiates a relationship by spending time with each other. Spending time together causes the emotion-called-love to eventually develop. In truth, the relationship can even take place over the phone or the Internet, since it is *time spent* that is important. Obviously, however, being together physically is the better choice.

The goal of step five is simply to increase the amount of time spent with each other. In so doing, generally, the people involved decrease the amount of time spent with other people. (In our society the word romance suggests a "couple" and excludes others.) It is this double-whammy effect that leads to the emotion-called-love.

Incidentally, the first date with someone can often determine whether there will even be a second date. As a result, most couples are on their best behavior during those first dates. Yet, in spite of their attempts to put their best collective feet forward, they often find that things don't "click."

Believe it or not, an entire evening's success can be decided during the first few seconds of a date with someone new. Unless one seemingly little thing occurs during those seconds, the date can become one that doesn't "click" from the start. That little thing relates to whether or not physical contact is established between the couple. Should a man, for example, fail to reach out during those first few seconds and, in some way, touch the girl he is dating, an enormous and sometimes highly frustrating barrier can develop between them. This barrier can prevent future contact from occurring or, at least, can make future contacts much more difficult.

What is peculiar about the entire idea is that the "touch" doesn't have to be sexual in nature (and, in fact, it generally had better not be). Even holding a date's hand on the way to the car can be all that is necessary to prevent a barrier from being built. The point is that the sooner physical contact is made, the better things will go.

Think back to your younger days and the movie dates you went on. I remember feeling as if I should put my arm around my date while watching the movie. But alas, my arm always seemed to be in a state of rigor mortis because it seldom succeeded in making that bold move. In fact, during this painful process, both people can be very much aware of the barrier.

When I was a teenager, I had a good friend tell me that once, while he was slowly inching his arm around his date, she suddenly turned, looked at him, and told him to simply put his arm around her and get it over with. We were both shocked at how forward it seemed and yet, I was jealous of his good luck.

Truthfully, the longer one waits to make "the move," the harder it is to ever make it. Simply holding your date's hand or touching her lightly on the shoulder on the way from her house to the car can avoid the entire problem. Perhaps the rigor mortis might not be so severe in the theatre. This is, of course, based upon the assumption that there was an attraction in the first place. (Yet, agreeing to date someone seems to pre-suppose such an attraction.) Finally, it goes without saying that "the move" can be made by the fairer sex also and, from experience, I can state it is generally, greatly appreciated.

Establishing Habit

In order to guarantee complete success with this step, you must insert yourself into her schedule as often and as consistently as you can. At first, this may not be easy. Look at the schedule you outlined in step four. By analyzing her activities you should be able to find *openings* in which you can attempt to become part of her schedule. An *opening* is defined as a time in her life when she is doing nothing, but wishes that she were doing something; and/or when she is with no one, but wishes that she were with someone. I can give you a perfect example of this type of opening with the following story.

Several times in the past, I have acted as a coach for people who were trying to establish relationships with someone they found attractive. They would report to me regularly and tell me how the relationships were going, and I would give them advice on what to do. One such client had his eye on an extremely attractive and popular college coed. However, he was experiencing excessive frustration because she had so many dates he was convinced she wasn't even aware he was alive. Several times he had asked her out, only to be turned down because she already had a date.

If you have followed what has been written so far, you should be able to see that his problem was he didn't know her schedule. Consequently, I recommended that he go back to step four, observe her for a while, and map out her activities. I advised him not to seek her company as a date for at least two or three weeks—not until he had step four completed. He spent nearly a month observing her and then brought the results to me. We sat down and discussed them.

He had a right to be frustrated. The girl was so busy with school, sorority life, and dating that it was unreal. In one month, she must have had dates with at least ten different guys. I felt if he wanted a date, he would have had to book her two to three weeks in advance. Hopeless? Not really. Just harder, that's all.

In looking over her schedule, we began to search for openings. At first none appeared, at least none that could be counted on. Eventually we found one—Sunday mornings. For some reason, Sunday mornings were completely empty.

Now that he had an opening, the challenge became how to insert himself into that time period. Ideally, they should be doing something pleasurable. And so the questions came: What can you do on a Sunday morning? Church? Naturally! But conversations with her led him to believe she wasn't religious; therefore, she might not get any pleasure out of church. How about sports? Usually a perfect idea! Yet, we decided that after her busy week she would probably rather slow down and relax on Sundays.

What then? Finally, something I remembered from my own college days gave us the answer: *sororities don't serve meals on Sundays*. That was it! Invite her out for a casual meal at a local restaurant. It was worth a try.

And so, he did. And she accepted. And they began going out *every* Sunday. And soon they were dating regularly. And, finally, they were going together. Ultimately, he introduced step seven— and they were in love.

The goal of step five is to insert yourself into your future lover's schedule as often and as consistently as you can. You are trying to set yourself up as a *habit*, by doing things on schedule. For example, every night you call at seven, or, as in the example above, every Sunday you go out to breakfast. With the modern invention called the cell phone and Internet dating opportunities, this task is even easier. Calling or e-mailing someone every day during a coffee break is way too easy compared to the olden days. And doing so can become a *pleasant habit*—one that both people look forward to.

Ideally, you should establish several times each day where your actions together become habitual. These times don't have to be very long; just three or four minutes at some time during the day can have great value if those minutes are habitual. *Habit creates expectancy, which is the whole idea.*

Sometimes establishing a relationship with someone takes a great deal of ingenuity and effort. I have known high school and college students who have scheduled their entire lives around the lives of their hopeful lovers. They have taken courses in school they didn't need, bought things they couldn't use, played sports they didn't like—all in an attempt to establish a relationship.

As I mentioned earlier, if you are a gorgeous person all this effort and plotting may not be necessary. However, if you are average looking, this probably makes sense to you—especially if your sights are set on someone you deem to be more attractive than yourself.

Keep in mind that should you be bold enough to set your sights too high, be prepared to be frustrated. While I believe in the power and potential of the seven-step formula, I don't see it as being supernatural. If you are plain looking, you are in for a major challenge if you set your sights on someone who is extremely attractive. Not that it isn't possible, mind you. It is! However, you'll have to have a fantastic personality, a lot of money, or something else going for you before it will work. And then, it won't be easy.

You might be lucky enough to locate a gorgeous soul who is lonely. Your chances of starting a relationship might be much better under those circumstances. Then again, to imagine a lonely gorgeous person is difficult. But—as strange as it may seem—there actually are gorgeous lonely people out there. You see—sometimes attractive people are so intimidating that everyone is *afraid* to ask them out. So, take a deep breath and get on the phone. You might get lucky.

Phylocs

There is a concept I have given the shortened name *phyloc*. Phyloc (pronounced *fi'-lock*) is short for *physical location*. I always tell people that while doing their research, they should pay strict attention to their hopeful lover's phylocs. His phylocs are important when trying to insert yourself into his schedule.

Suppose a lady is interested in a gentleman who works in the same office building as she does. After she has completed step four, she should have a chart that gives details about his phylocs. His daily phyloc schedule might look like the chart at the top of page 72.

This conceptualization of phylocs has obvious advantages. Since she knows he eats lunch every day at noon at Pete's Diner and walks from the office to Pete's, she could "accidentally" be walking down that same sidewalk toward Pete's at precisely the same time, making bumping into him practically unavoidable.

Other people may eat lunch with him, which is okay; however, once you have established a habit of meeting for lunch, you should attempt to get him away from everyone else. Try suggesting the two of you try a different restaurant. Watch it, though. You'll have to be prepared to respond in case he happens

Phyloc	Home	Office Break	Coffee	Office	Lunch
Phyloc to Phlyoc	7:15 bus from corner of 5th and Elm Street	Elevator to cafeteria at 10:15 AM	Elevator to office at 10:47 AM	Elevator at noon to 1st Floor, then by foot to Pete's	By foot at 12:55 to elevator, up to office, etc.

to refuse your invitation. If he does, I suggest you stammer a little and then say something like "Yikes! If you don't want to go with me, I sure don't want to go alone. I hate eating lunch alone. Besides, maybe good old Pete will have his chicken special today." Then change the subject and run along to lunch with him.

In laying out your plans you must realize that schedules are of several types: a daily schedule, a weekly schedule, a weekend schedule, and even a monthly schedule. Phyloc charts should be drawn up for each type. You can then establish habits in each of these time frames. Perhaps you could set it up to call every night (daily schedule), go bowling every Tuesday (weekly schedule), date in an official capacity on Friday and Saturday nights (weekend schedule), and attend the monthly meeting of the flying club together (monthly schedule).

To be truly effective with step five, two things must occur: you must become part of his schedule *and* other people must be eliminated from his schedule. The more success you have with these two points, the more intense the emotion-called-love will be once it occurs.

The success of this step, plus the effective use of step seven, actually combines to create the emotion-called-love. The interaction of these two steps determines the intensity of that emotion.

In the average love relationship, one in which both parties are enjoying themselves, these two criteria are almost imperceptibly satisfied. As the relationship develops, the couple finds they spend more and more time together and less time with others. Usually this is exactly what they want.

This is especially obvious when sex is involved. New sexual relationships tend to make a love addiction all too easy. No matter what level of sexual activity, from innocent, bashful, awkward touches to full-blown lust, the desire to be with your lover can consume your entire soul. Testosterone is a difficult hormone to ignore. Consequently, establishing habits in order to complete this step is usually quite simple.

Once patterns have been established, the couple begins to use words and phrases that describe the status of their relationship. These phrases are useful in advising other people how to act around them. For instance, the phrase "going steady" implies two people who are "going together" are "committed" to each other and so "involved" with each other that they are unavailable to date others. Those words have the impact of telling other people to stay away. (In similar fashion, the words *engaged* and *married* carry an even stronger warning to others.)

At this point, the emotion-called-love may not yet have developed. Love as pleasure has existed from the start, but until the emotion shows itself, the people involved might not say they are "in love." They might say they love each other's company—but aren't yet "*in love.*"

Usually step five doesn't take this much work and analysis. Falling in love is a smooth process that occurs naturally and almost unnoticeably. If the people who are dating are enjoying the relationship, they begin to seek each other's companionship at every possible opportunity.

In fact, you could say that once you start the ball rolling, it's harder to stop it than it is to keep it going. (The way our society is organized, most people need more companionship and affection than they have, making it likely they are willing to fall in love. They don't feel trapped at all—they feel honored and even lucky.)

One woman I was dating said, "Come on over, there's nobody home."
I went over—nobody was home.
Rodney Dangerfield

Step Six: Assessment of Progress

Love is nothing else but an insatiable thirst of enjoying a greedily desired object.

Montaigne, *Essays*

Well, we're getting there, slowly but surely. Thus far you have completed five steps: established your goals (step one), met the person (step two), felt and created an attraction (step three), observed and learned about the person (step four), and created time dependency (step five). If things are progressing well, you could say that you are falling in love. Not *in* love, but rather *falling* in love.

Steps six and seven usually take care of themselves at this point, and the people find themselves emotionally in love. However, since they don't always do so, I will continue.

Step six is simple enough. It involves an analysis of how the relationship is going. I have developed a method of figuring out how things are going by using mathematics. You actually count points and come up with a total.

There are three ways to get points:

1. You get one point for every minute you are together (as a habit, excluding others, if possible).

2. You get one point for every minute your lover is thinking about you and only you.

3. You get one point for every minute your lover is spending time doing something for you.

Since each day has twenty-four hours with sixty minutes per hour, by multiplying those together you get 1,440 possible points per day. Should your lover spend every minute of his life either with you, thinking about you, or doing something for you, then you could score 1,440 points per day. That would be the ideal. Realizing, of course, that the ideal can seldom be achieved, the goal is still to acquire as many points as possible. The more points you acquire, the more *time dependent* on you he becomes. The more time dependent he becomes, the more he *needs* you during those times.

In counting your points, you will encounter difficulty with the last two types. How often a lover is thinking about you or doing something for you is something you can only estimate. However, by asking your lover's friends or relatives, or even just paying attention to what he says or does, you can get a rough estimate of the points.

Suppose a man's lover shows up unexpectedly one day with cookies she has baked for him. He can be sure he acquired points while she was baking the cookies; how many can only be an estimate. Similarly, if a woman's lover calls her on the phone or looks her up frequently, she can be certain that she is getting many points between and during those times. Once you can socially apply any of the phrases that we mentioned earlier (*committed, going together, involved,* etc.), then you can safely say you have completed step six. I would estimate four or five hundred points per day would be adequate before moving on to step seven, especially if your lover has eliminated other people from his life during the times you are acquiring the points.

Time Dependency

One of the best quotes about love is at the beginning of this section by Lucretius (99-55 B.C.). He observed: "Habit causes love." In a way, he hit the nail on the head—and yet he lived several thousand years ago. I say "in a way" because I believe he should have said: "Habit causes the emotion-called-love."

Once we are involved in a habitual relationship, an emotional attachment is not too far away. In order to describe this phenomenon with words, I created the concept of "time dependency." Since habits are established using the ticking of the proverbial clock, the resulting relationships seem to be appropriately described as being ones that are caused by time itself. Thus, when we come to expect our lovers to call at an *exact point* in time, we could easily be described as being "time dependent" on that person for our habitual fix. If the anticipated phone call comes as scheduled, we are gleeful. Should the call be late, we feel uneasy—as if something were amiss. Consequently, it looks as if we are in love.

Time dependency is not only important in an analysis of love, it is also important in other areas of life. How time dependent a person is on others can determine how emotionally secure he is. This concept is extremely important in the rearing of children because it may be the main determining factor in the development of their personalities, not only as children, but also as adults. (But alas, that is the subject of another book.)

A date is a job interview that lasts all night. The only difference between a job interview and a date is that there are not many job interviews where there's a chance you'll end up naked at the end of it.
Jerry Seinfeld

Step Seven: Creating the Emotion-Called-Love

You must anger a lover if you wish him to love.
Publilius Syrus, *Sentenial*

The only ingredient missing in our imaginary relationship is the emotional aspect of love. Some relationships go along smoothly for months, during which time both people only experience a lot of pleasure—until step seven sneaks its way into the relationship, love can be all fun and games.

However, the peculiar thing is that the two people involved, although they may be treating each other beautifully and enjoying each other immensely, may still feel that they are not in love. According to the concepts in the first part of this book, they probably, logically, should be in love. The problem is they don't *feel* anything for each other (except rotten, old, nasty pleasure). Although they may be *involved*, they don't believe themselves to be *emotionally* involved.

A conversation that has occurred perhaps millions of times between a lover and her best friend goes something like this:

Friend: Well! How are you and Tom getting along?

Lover: Fantastically! Last night we went out to dinner and then afterward we went dancing. I had a marvelous time. He is so much fun!

Friend: (*teasing*) You can't fool me. I'll bet you're in love with him.

Lover: Oh! No! No! I'm not in love with him. Now, don't get me wrong. I like him very much, but I don't think I'm in love with him.

Friend: Don't expect me to believe that! All I've heard for the past three months is Tom this and Tom that. He's the only thing you think about any more.

Lover: (*thoughtfully, slowly, wonderingly*) I know! But I still don't feel I'm in love with him.

In Love

Okay, the stage is set! Our lover in the above example should be in love, but she isn't! She should feel emotional about her lover, but she doesn't! What the heck is missing? What must a lover do to feel the emotion-called-love?

You have probably guessed the answer to the puzzle already. I gave a perfect hint at the beginning of this step with the quote from Mr. Publilius. Unfortunately, the reason you may know the answer is because you have experienced the detestable emotion in the past. What causes this emotion to suddenly appear? Problems, just problems. Problems of any type and of any sort. As Publilius says—a little anger will work miracles. All that is needed for our lover in the example above to become emotional about Tom is for her to spot Tom talking with some other cute girl. Bingo! Instant emotion!!! And, if we were to maliciously want to make the emotion more intense, all we would have to do is let her spot Tom actually kissing the other girl! Ouch!!!

How many times have you seen this happen? How many times have you played the role of the lover in just such a circumstance? If, in real life, you have ever been in love, you probably didn't need to be told what step seven is. You've experienced step seven before, firsthand. We can all sense that *the emotion-called-love begins when something threatens a time-dependent relationship.*

The Unwritten Formula

Somewhere in our culture is an unwritten formula for how we will "just know" when we are in love. I have no idea who created the formula, but it has been lurking in the relationship shadows forever. I can hear a young girl asking her mother about love, with her final question being: "But, Mommy. How will I know when I am in love?" The mommy's response has always been: "Don't worry, sweetheart. You'll just know!"

This hidden secret to love turns out to be none other than an instantaneous upset feeling that occurs whenever a time-dependent relationship is threatened. Was Mommy referring to heartbreak? I think she was. After all, if she had been referring to Sexual Love or Attachment Love it wouldn't be such a mystery. No, indeed! She is referring to the feelings associated with *losing* someone who has been giving you pleasure and upon whom you have become time dependent as a result.

> This hidden secret to emotional love turns out to be none other than an instantaneous upset feeling that occurs whenever a time-dependent relationship is threatened.

Look at the conversation between a lover and her best friend. I doubt anyone who reads that text would argue with her when she stated she didn't feel she was in love with Tom. Why is that?

Suppose the two of them are extremely attracted to each other and have been enjoying incredible sex together. Why aren't they both willing to say I love you? What are they waiting for? I would wager that during their lovemaking, blood tests could isolate not only the sex hormone testosterone, but also many of the attachment hormones, like oxytocin and vasopressin. After months of dating, they undoubtedly have a great deal of affection for each other. So, why won't they say I love you?

They're waiting for something to happen, aren't they? They are waiting for that certain something Mother referred to years ago. Let's see if we can force those precious words out of one of them by *creating* the desired emotion many call *love*.

Getting to I Love You

Imagine a time-dependent relationship centered on lunch. A simple phone call can cause the emotion-called-love to occur. To demonstrate how predictable this is, our goal will be to create the emotion at exactly 11:46 a.m. Consequently, one should begin dialing the phone at 11:44 a.m. When your lover answers, use this conversation as your pattern.

Bob: Hello.

Susan: Hello, Bob. This is Susan.

Bob: Well, good morning, sweet Sue! How's my favorite girl today?

Susan: Oh! I'm fine, but …

Bob: (*Interrupting*) Wow! It's almost time for lunch, isn't it? Where shall we go today?

Susan: Well! That's what I'm calling about. I don't think I'm going to go today. (*Time: 11:45—better hurry, Sue.*)

Bob: Why not, sweetie? Is something wrong? Are you sick or something?

Susan: No! It's not that, or anything like that. It's just that I don't think I should go to lunch or anywhere else with you any more.

Bob: (*Emotionally, of course. His heart instantly went berserk.*) WHAT?

Susan: Well, Bob. I've been thinking about us a lot lately; that's all (*Time: 11:45 and thirty seconds*) and I have decided that our relationship isn't going anywhere. I hope you can understand what I mean.

Bob: Oh! I understand what you mean all right. I understand that you're being foolish too! Don't you know how much I love you? (*Time: 11:46— Congratulations, Sue.*)

I shall assume that I made my point with this example. The emotion-called-love occurs in one's body and it is under the control of another person. That other person can cause it to occur at any time. Time dependency is to blame.

The Emotion-Called-Love

I need to reiterate my views about emotional love. I don't like to call love an emotion. The rest of the world does; but I don't. My logic is simple. If, as I have concluded, love is a measurement of the pleasure one receives from a lover and if that is the only description of love I accept, then it only makes sense not to refer to the pain connected with love (caused by threats to the relationship) as being love. The pain is more descriptive of and caused by the *loss of pleasure*. The sequence is: Love—threat— emotion. Love *precedes* the emotion.

When Bob said "I love you," he did so because he was upset with Susan's remarks. He may indeed love her because of all of the pleasure he has been experiencing with her, though that isn't necessarily the case. Bob claimed love because he was upset. It would be less confusing if he were to realize he was upset because he loved her and it looked as if he might be losing the pleasure she was providing (a subtle but important difference).

In too many time-dependent relationships (especially long-term ones) neither partner is experiencing much pleasure from the circumstances they are in. Truthfully, some couples nearly hate each other and yet—the emotion will still show up whenever the future of the relationship is threatened. Time dependency demands it. (Sometimes physical dependency helps it along too.)

Therefore, when I refer to the emotion-called-love I do so because the rest of the world has classified love as being an emotion. When you see that phrase you will know I prefer not to use love in connection with emotion.

By pointing out how people end up in what can only be referred to as an "emotional love trap," the contents and explanations I have put forth convey a somewhat depressing and negative feeling about love itself. Ah, but hang in there with me. By understanding all of the pitfalls that lurk in romantic circles, you can gain a clearer view of what it takes to find and keep a healthy relationship; a goal all of us share.

Daniel: [To his ten-year-old stepson whose mother has recently died] *So, what's the problem, Sammy-o? Is it just Mum or is it something else? Maybe school? Are you being bullied? Or is it something worse? Can you give me any clues at all?*
Sam: *You really want to know?*
Daniel: *I really want to know.*
Sam: *Even though you won't be able to do anything to help?*
Daniel: *Even if that's the case, yeah.*
Sam: *OK. The truth is actually ... I'm in love.*
Daniel: *Sorry?*
Sam: *I know I should be thinking about Mum all the time, and I am. But the truth is, I'm in love and I was before she died, and there's nothing I can do about it.*
Daniel: *Aren't you a bit young to be in love?*
Sam: *No.*
Daniel: *Oh, OK, right. Well, I'm a little relieved.*
Sam: *Why?*
Daniel: *Well, you know—I thought it might be something worse.*
Sam: [incredulous] *Worse than the total agony of being in love?*
Daniel: *Oh. No, you're right. Yeah, total agony.*
From the movie Love Actually

CHAPTER 9

Rating Love Relationships: Does Your Love Rate a Perfect Ten?

"Love can find entrance not only into an open heart, but also into a heart well fortified, if watch be not well kept."

~ Francis Bacon, Essays of Love

NOW THAT WE HAVE REVIEWED THE FOUR TYPES OF LOVE, WE CAN look at relationships from a different perspective. An interesting exercise is to rate each of the four types based upon the characteristics of a given relationship.

Let's look at Sexual Love. Depending upon the level of sexual activity and desire, a man could rate his relationship on a scale from one to ten, with ten being the highest. For example, involvement in a twenty-year relationship wherein sex has become mundane, Sexual Love might earn a value of four or five. Likewise, no sexual activity in a relationship would rate a zero (or even a negative number); while lustful, passionate behavior would rate a ten. The number is indicative of the general satisfaction and behavior of the person doing the rating—a subjective and arbitrary factor indeed.

Obviously there are two points of view with each relationship, but for now, only one will be rated. Ultimately both sets of numbers should be compared and conclusions drawn.

The ideal love relationship would score perfect tens across the board, i.e., Sexual Love–10, Attachment Love–10, Intellectual Love–10, and Emotional Love–10. A ten in Sexual Love indicates the complete satisfaction of your needs in the most enjoyable way possible. In Attachment Love a ten indicates you thoroughly enjoy your partner and find no fault with him. Intellectual Love at ten implies happiness and general satisfaction. Finally, a rating of ten for Emotional Love indicates you are so in love as to be totally time dependent.

Although a perfect score of ten seems to be ideal; in the area of Emotional Love, a score of five is healthier. The time dependency factor should be minimized through effective life planning. Thus the ideal relationship is more like a 10, 10, 10, 5.

What can this chart reveal about a relationship, as scored by an imaginary man? Let's say he rates the relationship 10, 3, 3, 3. Hmm—wonderful sex with a woman he has some affection for and who is indeed likable but yet is only a small part of his life.

Do you think those numbers indicate a great relationship? Perhaps they do for him, but what if the woman gave the relationship a 5, 8, 8, 8. Her numbers indicate okay sex (5); with a charming man (8); who is not only fun, likeable, and friendly (8); but also a person she might consider sharing the rest of her life with (8).

If these people don't converse about their relationship, do you see how much of a disparity *of expectation* there could be about

> If the two people involved don't converse about their relation-ship, do you see just how much of a disparity of expectation there could be about its future?

its future? Can you also see why even a casual remark that might threaten their relationship could create an intense emotional misunderstanding between them? Not knowing about her time dependency and being unaware of its consequences could lead to many problems.

Can you picture how upset she might be after some innocent but threatening remark? And how oblivious he may be to her reaction?

From that point on, their relationship will never be the same. Both people will be confused until they come to terms with each other's expectations, and how the relationship fits into the parameters they both set forth.

The Negative Numbers

Look at these chart numbers: -5, 8, 8, 5. It looks as if this relationship has a great deal of potential if the negative number can be made positive. If not, the frustration could eventually destroy the good parts too.

Dr. Laura Schlessinger, the radio personality, deals with this sort of circumstance in her book *The Proper Care and Feeding of Husbands*, which I highly recommend since it is not only factual but also useful in helping to maintain relationships.

These numbers describe someone very much in love but who is extremely dissatisfied sexually. This sort of thing happens frequently. After years of marriage and several children, not only does sexual desire wane but life gets so hectic there is neither time nor any inclination to have sex with one's partner. Sometimes this is okay with both people; but often it is not. As Dr. Laura points out, unless something is done, the marriage itself is at risk.

Using this chart regularly can encourage communication and promote serious discussions about your relationship. Couples could rate their relationship and then exchange numbers. The results might be interesting. If both parties were to agree to set emotion aside, they could examine the relationship intellectually and improve on it where needed.

Keep in mind that just about any combination is possible.

What sort of relationship would 0, -5, 5, 8 describe? My guess: someone with absolutely no sexual interest in his mate (0); who has lost all affection for her, to the point where he seriously dislikes her (-5); but who gets some sort of satisfaction (perhaps monetary) out of the relationship (5); and who stays around because time dependency (insecurity) causes him to be afraid to leave her (8).

There are undoubtedly thousands, perhaps millions, of such relationships in existence today.

All Relationships

If you think about the ideas behind the chart, it is apparent they can be applied to all relationships in life. I distinctly recall coming to the realization that I was extremely time dependent upon my first-born son when he was two years old. I was so taken by him I never could get enough of him. Using this chart I can now look at it from a view I didn't have back then. I think my chart would have looked like: 0,10,10,10. Obviously sexual love does not apply (0) but my affection and the pleasure I received from my son were completely off the charts (10), I was totally and absolutely happy with everything about him (10), and I was extremely time dependent on him (10) (an obvious exaggeration for the sake of the story).

Once when I took the little rascal shopping with me, he vanished in a department store. I had been looking for clothes in the men's area when I lost track of him. A quick search turned up nothing. I couldn't find him. In a split second, my brain reviewed the situation and imagined some evil person grabbing him and running out the door. My heart nearly came out of my chest. I began to run frantically around the store in a severe panic while calling for him. I was about to run outside in search of him when I thought I heard his sweet voice behind me. Sure enough, there he was, peeking out from between a couple of coats hanging on a rack. His blossom face looked so beautiful and innocent. I ran over and picked him up and nearly squeezed him in half. Tears came to my eyes because I felt such total relief at having found him. Time dependency is powerful.

Whenever I try to imagine what heartbreak feels like to others, I often refer back to that moment in order to identify with them. My time dependency on my young son caused all of those feelings. Still, knowing what I know, I wouldn't have wished otherwise. I was aware I was taking a serious emotional risk by being so attached to him, but he was worth it.

Thankfully, nothing has happened too seriously to any of my children. However, should something horrible occur, I know I will survive. I might need to become a tri-athlete in order to burn up all the energy within me, but I am prepared to do so. Thus, I feel I am stable enough to take time-dependent risks—mostly because of the thoughts contained in this book. Understanding the purpose and function of human emotions gives you power over them.

Doctor Marcia Fieldstone (a radio talk show host): *People who truly loved once are far more likely to love again. Sam, do you think there's someone out there you could love as much as your wife?* (Sam's wife has died)

Sam Baldwin: Well, Dr. Marcia Fieldstone, that's hard to imagine.

Doctor Marcia Fieldstone: What are you going to do?

Sam Baldwin: Well, I'm gonna get out of bed every morning . . . breathe in and out all day long. Then, after a while, I won't have to remind myself to get out of bed every morning and breathe in and out . . . and, then after a while, I won't have to think about how I had it great and perfect for a while.

Doctor Marcia Fieldstone: Tell me, what was so special about your wife?

Sam Baldwin: Well, how long is your program? Well, it was a million tiny little things that, when you added them all up, they meant we were supposed to be together . . . and I knew it. I knew it the very first time I touched her. It was like coming home . . . only to no home I'd ever known . . . I was just taking her hand to—to help her out of a car and I knew. It was like . . . magic.

From the movie *Sleepless in Seattle*

CHAPTER 10

Love's Intensity and Emotional Security: Does Passion Signal Security?

"Love is the tyrant of the heart; it darkens reason, confounds discretion; deaf to counsel. It runs a headlong course to desperate madness."

~ John Ford, The Lover's Melancholy

FOR YEARS I AGREED WHOLEHEARTEDLY WITH THE ABOVE QUOTE, because of my sad experience with love. Now, however, since the mental fog about love has lifted, I have a strong desire to simply correct him. You see, the truth is, he was confused. Love isn't the tyrant of the heart—emotion is! It's debilitating emotion that ruins everything. Thus, his quote should be altered to say: Emotion, caused by loss of love, is the tyrant of the heart. Love is innocent.

Time Dependency Discussed

The emotion-called-love can occur any time, as long as this formula is followed:

TIME DEPENDENCY + THREAT = EMOTION

I came up with the concept of time dependency as a result of some rather indirectly connected concepts in philosophy and physics. For years I had been fascinated with the characteristics and nature of time (especially from the viewpoint of Einstein and his theory of relativity) when, somewhere along the way, I concluded that the only true reality in nature is the present. The future and the past are mere fantasies created by the brain—to enhance our odds of survival. We create the past and the future (as if they were real) inside our heads. One could say that the past and the future are merely electro-chemical processes within us. They don't, therefore, exist separate from ourselves. The memories of past disasters plus the anticipation of future ones, give us an obvious *survival* advantage. This idea is consistent with our original outline and with survival being the main cause for all behavior.

From those conclusions, it was only a small step for me to realize that the main job or duty of the brain is to monitor time and to look for anything that might threaten our existence—which is exactly what is going on with time dependency.

The brain monitors the ticking of the clock in order to guarantee survival. It works to establish safe routines, avoiding any unnecessary risks in the process. In order to keep the body *safe in time*, it works hard to establish predictable safe routines of behavior. Once established, it doesn't take kindly to changes that might upset the apple cart (since the current situation is working). Even in an abusive relationship, the threat of emotional pain should the relationship end, outweighs the reality of the physical pain. This explains why people stay in these kinds of relationships. Whenever it appears as if survival is dependent upon one particular person, it only stands to reason that panic would occur over loss of that person.

The Generalization of Love

While at the beginning of a relationship very few things remind us of the person with whom we are becoming acquainted, eventually more and more objects in the environment become capable of turning our thoughts to that person. By the time a few months have passed, literally hundreds of things can remind us of our love. This occurs as a result of conditioning or learning, wherein the brain learns that the fulfillment of certain needs is dependent upon that person, making it important that the person be remembered.

In love, this conditioning process is an intriguing phenomenon in that, eventually, some of the most peculiar things will turn our thoughts to our loved one. Songs, cars, foods, movies, and hundreds of other items can have this affect. I was casually acquainted with a man who thought of his wife every time he saw a cow. Everyone thought this was rather humorous. She did not, of course. The explanation for the association was that her father was a rancher and, as a result, a great deal of their courtship took place out on the range where the two lovers frolicked among the cows.

This process is one of the many reasons people become time dependent on each other. Those objects that turn your thoughts toward your lover have the effect of giving your lover points. The more things in the environment that remind you of your lover, the more points he acquires. And interestingly, these reminders develop automatically as a result of experience, and their numbers are directly proportional to the amount of time you spend together. If you only ate at the local waffle house once with your lover, the waffle house probably won't remind you of him. However, if the waffle house becomes a part of your weekly schedule over an extended period, then not only will it remind you of him, but waffles themselves may serve as a reminder—along with the blueberry syrup that your lover loved on his waffles.

This snowball effect can eventually escalate to such proportions that almost everything in your life reminds you of the person you love. Such a situation usually occurs in marriages because of the amount of time most married couples spend with each other.

This phenomenon can cause you to chuckle, smile, and sigh at the realization of its workings. It is flattering to your lover when you tell him how many things remind you of him. However, the phenomenon can become frustrating should you desire to leave and forget your lover. Romances that last for years but then end for some reason (death, divorce) are examples of how these reminders can be the cause of much unhappiness. You will remain emotionally attached to your departed lover to the degree that those objects serve as reminders (points again). Should you never replace your lover with other people or another lover, this emotion can last for years. Under these circumstances, the emotion connected to love could last forever, just as the fairy tales claim. Time dependency is at work again.

Man's Imagination—A Blessing or a Curse?

The brain constructs its own reality by creating vivid pictures of the past and the future. We refer to these pictures as our imagination. The ability to picture or imagine future events allows us to change our behavior in order to, for example, avoid a dangerous situation. We have undoubtedly survived as a species because of our ability to imagine what the past and future hold.

But alas, a problem developed as a result. As fascinating as this sounds, only the intellectual portion of the brain (the cerebral cortex) can separate imagination from reality. *The primitive part of the brain absolutely believes everything the imagination dreams up.* That has led to our exasperating ability to ruin or enhance present time (the only true reality) by imagining things that are *not real* in the supposed past or future. Some things imagined are fun—some make us miserable. I could list millions of such nonsensical examples.

A person who is afraid to fly across the country has undoubtedly imagined what could happen if the plane were to crash. That vivid imagination has resulted in a fear of flying because the primitive brain pictures the plane in the process of crashing.

In a love relationship, one's imagination can convince the primitive brain that the loved one is, for example, more a part of life than he really is. That, of course, leads to time dependency, which leads to emotion.

Cassandra

I must confess to having experienced a time-dependent relationship with a dog at one point in my life. Since many people have experienced the same thing, my story might be helpful in understanding time dependency.

I started a job in a new town and therefore knew few people my own age. Coincidentally, a girlfriend had recently given me a cute German shepherd puppy. Since puppies require a lot of care, I found myself spending most of my non-working hours with Cassandra. She was my entertainment and companion. I acquired no new "after-work" friends during this time and, as a result, you could say I became *after-work time dependent* on my puppy. (This was long before I had come up with my theories about love, so I wasn't prepared for what was to come.)

One day when I came home from work, Cass wasn't in the yard where she should have been. I freaked out! I lost it. I drove around town until the wee hours of the morning looking for her, and I distinctly remember shedding tears and thinking the end of the world was near. I was obviously overreacting. Or was I?

In retrospect, I don't suppose I was, really! In fact, I was behaving normally and predictably. Think about it. Go back to the formula at the beginning of this chapter. Time dependency plus threat equals emotion. I was time dependent on Cass and she was lost. The ultimate threat! Thus—emotion!

Thankfully I found her. Would you believe that the pain I experienced while Cass was lost turned out to be one of the keys to the formula for love? At the time, I remember comparing my feelings to when girls had callously dumped me—especially the previously mentioned high-school sweetheart. I realized even then that the emotions were *identical. Absolutely identical!*

Emotional Security

A person is time dependent on another person to the degree that he is *involved* with that person. The level of involvement is determined by how much time is actually spent thinking about the other person, doing something for him or being with him (our point system). Incidentally, the best way to look at those three ways of acquiring points is to count the amount of "brain time" spent on the individual.

However, there is another important factor in the point system. In order to be sure of your points, others must be excluded from your lover's life. It is this aspect I will deal with now.

Each of us has needs and desires we are constantly trying to satisfy. Many of our needs can only be satisfied by other people and, to the degree that this is true, you could say we need others. We need to be accepted by others and told we are okay; we need to be liked by others and be sought after by them; we need to talk to others, to touch others, to enjoy others. Social anthropologists maintain that many of these needs are universal in nature and all humans have them. To the degree this is true, you can say these needs are instinctive.

In everyday life, we all search for others who can satisfy our needs. Should we find someone who satisfies those needs, we express feelings of happiness. This is exactly what occurs in a love relationship. Ideally, each person in the relationship satisfies the needs of the other. To the degree they succeed in doing so, they are happy. As we have seen earlier, the problem arises when the satisfaction of those needs is somehow threatened. *A person who needs another too much is happy only as long as that other is available.* The emotion will strike as soon as the "need satisfier" is lost. This emotion can be called love, but it can also be referred to as unhappiness. Love seems like a trap that must eventually lead to this unhappiness (even if everything goes beautifully for years; death itself can end the relationship and cause unhappiness). Is this unhappiness inevitable? *Indeed it is, as long as the lovers are time dependent.*

The solution to the problem could be summarized using some sage advice from Grandmother. "Don't," she advises, "put all your eggs into one basket. If you should lose that basket, you lose all." People who are in love are going against Grandmother's advice. *Too many of their needs are being satisfied by one person.*

After contemplating the concept of time dependency for several years, I came up with the following formulas for life in general:

You + many people = emotional security

And

You + too few people = emotional insecurity

Looking at the phrase "emotional security," it is important to note that the idea is really to keep one *free from negative emotions*. That belief is based upon the fact that true negative emotions are symptomatic of an unhappy state of being. All of us avoid negative emotions like the plague. In fact, not only do we avoid them, we avoid all things and all people who cause such negative feelings in us.

Based upon the formula, we can conclude that since each of us has needs that can be satisfied only by other people, then it stands to reason the more people there are to satisfy those needs, the better off we'll be. Thanks Grandma!

> Living life to its fullest is more likely if our friends are numerous.

Casual Versus Intimate Relationships

I think it pertinent to point out that most of the relationships you maintain with others will be of the more casual type. We all need to have many friends if we are to ever be satisfied with life. Living life to its fullest is more likely if our friends are numerous.

I simply maintain that it is better to have, for example, an entire list of golf buddies rather than a few favorites. Naturally some are favorites but if one feels like playing golf on a particular day, having to rely on a few favorites in order to get up a game is perhaps not the best plan.

Similarly, many of us prefer to be with someone when we go into a restaurant or other public place. If we don't have someone with us, we feel as if everyone else is staring at us. While we might be able to handle the staring, we become self-conscious when we imagine the thoughts that might be going through the minds of the patrons as they look at us. Perhaps we are afraid they feel sorry for us because we are alone, which means that no one likes us. As a result, many people choose to avoid such situations and do not go out alone.

Thus, the more people you know and are friends with, the more likely you are to have your needs satisfied, whatever they may be. And, in as much as your needs have the potential to be satisfied in the future, you feel secure. Perhaps security is simply the knowledge that no matter what you may need in the future, someone will always be willing to satisfy that need.

Maybe that's what love is all about—we have a guaranteed satisfier of our needs available whenever we may need him. This gives us a feeling of security. But are we really secure under these circumstances? *No! We are not!* We may feel secure at the time, but in reality it is a "sandy security;" a security that may look and feel good but one that is built without a firm base. *As soon as the lover leaves, the security crumbles.*

This idea applies to all other phases of life also. Security is having ten sources of income. Security is having twenty bowling buddies. Security is having ten girlfriends. Security is having dozens of close friends. Security is having fifty warm blankets. (Take note here, Linus.)

Ultimately the reason why these are good definitions for security lies in the fact that should you have, for example, many warm blankets, when Lucy or Snoopy steals one, you won't even notice it is gone. You can snub your nose at their futile attempts to upset you, because you are secure. Admittedly, however, the insecurity of having only one blanket *might* be better than the insecurity of having none. I used the word might because it seems logical that the more you have, the more you have to lose. And the more you *need* the things you have, the more upsetting will be their loss. Thus, if you don't even own a blanket, you will never become upset by its absence. A strange way of looking at it, don't you think?

However, in the game of love, as frustrating as it may be and from an emotional perspective only, a single person may actually be more secure emotionally than his married and therefore time dependent counterparts. Life may be less fulfilling in some areas perhaps but many are willing to make such sacrifices in order to avoid future, love caused, emotional states.

When it comes to relationships, some people are not capable of handling the risks associated with a strong time-dependent relationship. By absorbing yourself completely into a time-dependent relationship, you set yourself up for great upheaval and turmoil. In other words, my advice is to maintain relationships with your family and friends so you have more than one person to spend time with.

Why Time Dependency

Why do people allow themselves to become time dependent on only one person? It's undoubtedly because it is difficult enough to establish a relationship with one person without hoping for more. The social complexities and difficulties of dating, along with the moral complications involving sexuality, are the main causes for falling in love. It is much easier to allow yourself to become time dependent on the person you are dating than to be constantly looking for other dates and finding yourself alone, lonely and sexually frustrated when you fail. Finding new people to date and to share your company is hard work. It is so much easier simply to find someone you like and stick with him. At least you won't have to eat dinner alone so often.

From this lonely position in life, all one has to do is search for someone in a similar position, i.e., another lonely person. In all likelihood, should things go according to plan, a love relationship might be the result. In a very real sense, following this plan is at times highly practical. When two lonely people fall in love, two happy people can be the result, and it is difficult to improve on happiness when compared with loneliness. There are, however, several things to keep in mind in this regard.

First, while finding someone to love may solve the issue of loneliness, it also creates several new problems of its own. Loneliness is usually easier to handle than feelings connected with loss. When two lonely people fall in love, that love becomes *extremely* important to them. Therefore, should the relationship fail, its failure can be catastrophic.

The loss is often viewed as the loss of all meaning for life. Again, time dependency and its resulting emotional state are to blame. Unfortunately, there is simply no way around the problem. Because of the tentative nature of life itself, all love relationships must eventually end; it cannot be prevented. Only the degree of the resulting emotion can be controlled by the inclusion of others in your life. This can be more easily accomplished after a person who has had no one in his life finds someone, because that someone can serve to create more self-confidence and can act as a means of social support in future relationships.

One point I want to make here is that, as a couple, you should try to help each other establish relationships with other people. Force yourself to intentionally spend less time alone and more time in the company of relatives and friends. This is much easier when two people support each other in this endeavor.

A person alone may feel helpless and afraid to venture out into the world, but a person in love should find the task much easier. Dinner dates; evenings playing cards; going to movies, sporting events, and the like are all occasions that lend themselves to group participation. The friendships one acquires during such activities can serve to expand the happiness one feels.

Can you imagine how the pioneers must have felt when loved ones died? Many lived on farms located miles from anyone else. Consequently, the time dependency within the family was total—1,440 points. If one's spouse were to die under those circumstances, the resulting emotion for the survivors would obviously be extreme. That's undoubtedly why so many of them were described as having lost their minds upon the death of a spouse. Extreme emotion is tough to deal with.

A pessimist is a man who thinks all women are bad; an optimist is one who hopes they are.
Chauncey M. Depew

CHAPTER 11

Additional Thoughts on Time Dependency: Topsy-Turvy Love

*"And how can curses keep him yours
when kisses could not make him so?"*

~ Anne Goodwin Winslow

THE EMOTION-CALLED-LOVE IS CREATED BY TIME DEPENDENCY. If, as a society, we could discontinue referring to love as an emotion, the confusion about the word would be reduced. Perhaps we could refer to the emotion-called-love as "separation anxiety" (the same as in child psychology—used whenever a child cries when separated from his mother). *Anxiety* is a more accurate description of reality. (I appropriately used the word *depression* in the first chapter when describing my feelings after my high-school relationship ended. I doubt anyone caught the significance of it at the time. Hopefully it makes sense now.)

By changing our approach to love, we can eliminate several other confusing things. Let's begin with two quick statements:

1. Love is positively correlated to pleasure.

2. Time dependency disrupted causes the emotion that society calls love.

If you understand these two statements, you should be able to identify with my objections to situations wherein people claim to be in love and yet give no evidence of it in their *behavior*.

I once knew a married couple that constantly fought whenever they were together. These fights weren't mere lovers' quarrels either; they were downright nasty. More than once each of them required medical attention after one of their bouts. Luckily, they weren't together too often since the husband worked long hours on his job and would seldom go home after work. He usually stopped for a beer or two (or twenty) at the local tavern. More often than not, that is where his wife would find him, at which point the fighting would begin.

Her days were spent at home watching their two kids and taking care of the house. She rarely went anywhere except to the laundry or grocery store. When she did manage to leave the house, naturally she had to take the kids with her.

One night, during one of his many drunken escapades, he managed to kill himself in a car wreck. Considering the circumstances, it takes no genius to know that this woman was going to experience an extreme emotional reaction upon his death. While it seems peculiar that she would be time dependent on him, she had no other adult relationships to divide her dependency amongst. She was financially dependent *and* time dependent upon him and, as a consequence, she predictably experienced severe emotional trauma when he died. The frustrating aspect of this whole story is that she called the emotional reaction "love" and, since it was a severe reaction (for she was extremely time dependent upon him), she and her friends maintained that she loved him *deeply*.

Although it's not my position to determine she didn't love him; from all that was apparent, it is difficult to imagine how love was even a possibility. They fought constantly when they were together, so it is hard to imagine how she could have been getting much pleasure out of the relationship. It is my contention that the emotion she felt had very little to do with love. She was, simply, too dependent upon him for her survival. When he was killed, her body panicked and began to fear for her future survival.

This is why I don't like love being called an emotion. Why would we ever want to waste the word when describing nasty hateful relationships? The love these folks describe as being a part of their relationship undoubtedly had very little to do with pleasure. It makes no sense to claim that you love someone who constantly mistreats you or to say you love someone you despise or are repulsed by. I can make it even simpler than that. How can people ever claim to love someone they don't even *like*? It's foolishness!

Every time I observe dysfunctional relationships, it turns out that time dependency and the resulting emotion are responsible for any profession of love between the two people. *If there is no logically motivated selflessness or pleasure-connected affection between people, I refuse to use love to describe the relationship.*

What people in dysfunctional relationships need to realize is that time dependency causes them to *fear* losing their current relationship. They probably aren't staying together because they are in love. They are staying together for some reason other than love. Perhaps money, sex, or children are keeping them in the relationship.

> It makes no sense to claim that you love someone who constantly mistreats you or to say you love someone you despise or are repulsed by.

In relationships experiencing emotional difficulties, the people involved have a hard time understanding personal feelings. This confusion creates severe communication barriers. Trying to resolve disagreements is then difficult.

Love's Flawed Logic

A similar problem in logic occurs in the reverse. People who don't experience an emotion in connection with love are prone to believe that no love is present in the relationship. Extremely busy professionals often face this dilemma. Some travel extensively and are, therefore, too busy to be time dependent on anyone. I suspect such is often the case in Hollywood when both people have successful separate careers.

I once taught psychology to two young people who were going steady while they were in my class. They married about a year later. I always thought they made a perfect couple. They seemed happy when they were together and appeared to be very much in love with each other. When I heard that they were married, I felt sure the marriage would be a happy one.

For several years I heard nothing from them, until one day they both came into my office to seek some advice. They were considering getting a divorce and wanted to know what I thought about the idea. We met several times that week to talk about the situation. After a number of discussions with both of them and one or two sessions with each one individually, I still couldn't figure out why they were thinking about a divorce. As far as I could ascertain, they got along beautifully. Their finances were sound, their lifestyle was comfortable, and even their sex life was satisfying. It all boiled down to a conclusion that they were no longer in love.

The idea seemed crazy to me. Here were two lovable people (both admitted that they were being treated very well by the other and they still *liked* each other) with what appeared to be a perfect marriage—contemplating a divorce.

Finally, during a discussion with the young woman, she casually made the comment that all the pizzazz was gone from their marriage. Now, the word *pizzazz* implied one of two things to me: either the pizzazz in their sex life had faded (a common complaint) or *pizzazz* referred to the emotion-called-love. Since we had previously established that sex was not the issue, I turned my attention to the emotional aspects of their relationship.

Upon being questioned, the woman stated that lately she never got too excited about seeing or not seeing her husband. She said when they were first married, she couldn't stand to be away from him and often cried whenever she wasn't able to be with him. Now, although she still enjoyed his company, she didn't miss him and, in fact, they didn't see each other nearly as much as before.

It was this last comment that started me thinking that perhaps their problem was one involving a change in their time-dependent schedule. This phenomenon occurs frequently in love relationships and can cause subtle problems. When two people first begin to date, they spend a great deal of time together *alone*. However, after several years of marriage, many couples spend more time with their friends and in other activities (which is exactly what I recommend). As a result, they become less time dependent upon each other. *Now, since the level of one's time dependency determines the intensity of the emotion connected to love, it sometimes appears to the people involved that they are literally falling out of love since they no longer feel as emotional.*

In the case of this young couple, the level of time dependency had significantly decreased. Both of them had full-time jobs they enjoyed. They were only together in the evenings for a few hours before going to bed. What is also significant is that during the day they were both constantly coming into contact with many other people because of their jobs. This all added up to a decrease in their time dependency on each other and a subsequent decrease in the level of their *emotional* love. This decrease was so dramatic that they actually began to feel as if they didn't love each other any more.

After I pointed this out to them, they agreed that the whole problem appeared to be they believed love was an emotion in the first place. They also began to realize they did love each other because they still enjoyed each other's company when they were together.

Essentially what this young couple was telling me was that they weren't happy unless they were sad. Unless you cry yourself to sleep in someone's absence, it is impossible to be happy in his presence.

The type of relationship this young couple shared is the type of relationship I value the most. There is nothing more beautiful to behold than seeing two people who really are in love. This couple had an enjoyable and pleasurable relationship—without negative emotion—that could last for many years. In order to get the pizzazz back into their relationship, they needed to focus on putting more of the pleasures they shared back into their daily lives. They simply didn't appreciate how great it was. Remember what Shakespeare said: *"Love moderately; Long love doth so."*

Love Versus Other Emotions

Interpreting one's feelings once a time-dependent relationship falls apart is difficult. People in love can be so confused they don't know if they are experiencing love or some other emotion.

Suppose a woman has been suddenly jilted by her lover of two years upon whom she had been very time dependent. She may be so hurt that she can't exactly interpret her feelings. She finds herself saying things like "I *hate* him for what he has done to me. Doesn't he know how much I *love* him? Every time I think about it I get *angrier* and *angrier*, and whenever I see him with that new girlfriend of his I get so *jealous* I could just cry." She's emotionally confused, wouldn't you say?

Trying to decide why this is even possible has led me to some rather unusual conclusions. Try following this next section while applying the ideas to your life.

A Closer Look

It is my conclusion, after years of research, that *all* negative emotions are the same biologically. They only vary according to the intensity of the internal upheaval and the circumstances that caused the upheaval in the first place. As far as I am concerned, psychologists and others are wasting their time when they try to *biologically* differentiate between anger, hatred, depression, anxiety, or any other negative emotion. Except for the variation in cause and effect, there is no difference. The primitive brain, which controls those responses, is not so sophisticated as to be able to differentiate between the various possible (socially determined) emotional states.

Go back to our last example. The woman was jealous, angry, hateful, and in love—all at the same time. My point is this: *she* decides how to categorize her feelings. In trying to convey to us how she is interpreting her internal physical state, she simply chooses one of the many emotional words available to her. And it's amazing how many of those words will fit her situation. She can be angry, jealous, mad, upset, in love, full of anguish, distraught, or any other negative emotion. Isn't that peculiar?

All of those emotional words (and many more) fit her situation. *Nothing inside her body needs to have changed in order for her to switch words.* She can be jealous one second and angry the next. Could it be that the physiological symptoms of all of those negative emotions are the same?

In this lady's particular situation, we know what caused her to become emotional—her lover jilted her. What we don't know is how serious an emotion it is. How many and how intense are her emotional symptoms? A medical exam could help in this analysis by determining her heart rate, blood pressure, etc. The higher or more serious the symptoms, the more seriously she must have perceived the threat to be. It is my belief that the intensity of the emotion will vary on a scale that is directly related to time dependency. The more time dependent, the more serious the emotion; and vice versa.

If the emotion is intense enough it can lead to serious aggression. On any given day, we hear about people who have killed their lovers (or a third party) because they "loved them so much." Is the lady in our example a candidate for such rash behavior? Should her former lover (now known as the "big jackass") consider hiding out for a while? Maybe! Maybe not! What is fascinating in these cases is that should she do some evil thing to him, many people will identify and sympathize with her. Many times people have been acquitted when on trial for murdering their lovers because the juries "understood their motives." These violent acts are classified as "crimes of passion." The passion everyone is referring to is understood to be the emotional upheaval that occurs when we lose the person we love. Maybe we should try to control the intensity of the emotion as much as possible in the first place.

Rarely is a time-dependent lover willing to move on without

some sort of protest. Many hang on for dear life, with no intention of giving in. The situation is frustrating for both parties.

Love Hurts

People experiencing intense emotional upheaval commonly describe the feeling as one that hurts immensely. It hurts so much sometimes that murder and suicide seem to make sense—just to get rid of the pain. I have counseled many people about their love problems and an alarming number admitted suicide had crossed their minds.

Identifying with the hurt these people feel is difficult but, by referring to other intense emotions, an easy comparison can be made. Remember, I maintain that all negative emotions are essentially the same biologically. Only the intensity varies according to the circumstances that caused the arousal in the first place. Thus, *biologically speaking, the emotion we call love is essentially the same as the emotion we call fear, and the emotions we call anger, or hatred, or anxiety.*

Suppose someone has almost fallen off a tall building and just down the street an extremely time-dependent person has just been told his wife wants a divorce. Both people will respond emotionally: one with fear, the other with love or heartbreak.

Now, let's do something interesting. The *very second* the two emotions appear, let's freeze the action and allow a doctor to examine the two people in a neutral location. It is my contention the doctor will not be able to tell which person experienced which emotion. Their physical symptoms will be identical. (It is important to note that even ten or fifteen seconds after the initial emotional reactions, the internal symptoms of the two people may begin to show major variations. In this example especially, it is apparent that the person who nearly fell off the roof will undoubtedly begin to calm down more quickly than his counterpart because, for him, the danger is over.)

Try to recall when you have experienced a situation similar to the first person. Consider for a moment how intense your fear was. Now you should be able to identify with the victim of heartbreak. He is experiencing those exact symptoms, except his symptoms may not fade away for a long period of time. Can you imagine how you would feel if you were to experience that level of emotion for days or weeks on end?

That's why people behave so irrationally during these times. You simply have to do *something* when you feel that way. Regrettably, positive forms of adjustment are rare.

Why is it that a person experiencing heartbreak is advised to "grow up" or to "get over it?" Many people consider these reactions to be childish and immature. Yet, if someone was experiencing anxiety or depression (the same package of symptoms biologically), we might rush him to a doctor for treatment. Perhaps heartbreak should be taken more seriously. Readjustment takes time and the healing process can drag on and on. If we were to prescribe sedatives to victims of heartbreak, maybe the number of murders and suicides would be diminished.

Irrational Love

Sometimes sympathy for a person who has gone bonkers over another person isn't enough. These pitiful souls need to have a friend who will help them through the hurt. When you lose your mind over someone, all too often you actually feel as if something is mentally wrong with you. I've had people suffering from heartbreak tell me they thought they were going crazy. They see themselves as weak, useless, laughable human beings. How else could they defend their behavior? What other explanation is there for calling someone fifty times a day or driving past his house ten times an hour?

These people sense their behavior is unusual and are so embarrassed by it they keep their behavior a secret from everyone around them. When co-workers catch them daydreaming about their lovers they will deny it and claim to be thinking about something else. Truthfully, there is nothing wrong with them; they are as normal as the day is long.

Those who have never lost their minds over someone can take the superior attitude and believe the in-love types are weird because they behave so foolishly. Yet the feelings they experience could happen to any one of us given the right circumstances.

If you are reading this and you fit this description, take heart. You are not crazy or weak or weird. You do, however, need to resist behaving irrationally and get busy doing other things. Let time pass and you'll start feeling more in control.

Here's a bit of practical advice. If it is true that points given to your lover are exactly what is confusing the brain into believing that your lost love is so important to your happiness, then *stop giving away the points*. But, you ask, how can you do that successfully when you are currently thinking about your lover with every fiber of your soul?

In truth, it's not as tough as it may seem. You see, most of the time when you are moping over your lover, you are *concentrating* on your problem. It's simple! *Stop concentrating on your problems* and switch your focus to something else. Find things that are fun or stimulating to concentrate on. If you can do something with friends, that's even better. (Incidentally, the second you catch yourself feeling sorry for yourself, lamenting your fate, and looking for sympathy from your friends, reach up with your hand and slap yourself. Instead show a strong front to others and keep busy with something.)

I've given this advice many times, so I know it works. If you arrive home at night and immediately start to get those awful feelings when you sit down on the couch, get up immediately and grab a book or turn on the television or call someone. However, if you seek help from others, be careful not to talk about your love problems. Don't dwell on the things that upset you. Dreaming or talking about your lost love is sending points. Do something constructive. You simply have to *reverse your time dependency* or you may not feel normal again for a long time.

Lastly, the most practical advice of all: find a new lover!

Once a woman gives you her heart, you can never get rid of the rest of her.
John Vanbrugh

Love's Time Schedule: Predicting Love

"All love is vanquished by a succeeding love."

~ Ovid

MANY PEOPLE HAVE ASKED ME HOW LONG IT TAKES TO FALL IN love with someone. My answer is: "From the amount of time it takes to snap your fingers up to ten years or more, depending on the circumstances and people involved. The average, however, seems to be about six weeks."

Why do I say this? Let's examine the finger-snapping idea first. Remember that love *as an emotion* results from time dependency that has been disrupted. The question is, then, how long does it take for us to become time dependent on another person?

A handsome man or a beautiful woman could answer this. Attractive people undoubtedly have to be careful about whom they smile at. It may only take a casual smile from an attractive person to lure someone into falling in love with him instantly (all sex aside). The love can be very emotional too.

How is this possible? Consider our point system. Remember you acquire points according to how much time the person spends with you, thinks about you, or does something for you.

Admirers can become instantly time dependent after a smile because, from that moment on, their lives are consumed with thoughts about the other person—all of which give him points. The threat that is necessary to create the emotion is built into the situation because they don't stand a chance. There is no relationship in the first place. The frustration and general bad feelings they experience are frequently called love; though "love sickness" is a better term.

This type of love has been given several names. Since their love is foolish, it has been called *immature infatuation*; since it is unreturned, it has been called *unrequited love*; and since it happens so quickly, it has been called *love at first sight*. It should be noted that this love at first sight can be a sexless love—totally dissimilar to the love that develops at first sight because of pure physical sex appeal or attraction. The latter type of love is more appropriately entitled lust, *which causes many of us to fall in love daily*.

Now let's look at love that takes ten years or more to be realized. Again, I'll use an example to illustrate. William Makepeace Thackeray wrote one of my favorite love stories, *Vanity Fair*. As the novel ends, two of its main characters, Amelia Sedley and Major William Dobbins, get married. Throughout the book everyone knows that Major Dobbins loves Amelia. Everyone, that is, except Amelia. It takes eighteen years before she realizes it is Major Dobbins whom she has loved all along. She wasn't able to realize this until he left her (step seven). It was only after he was gone and she realized how much she needed him that she was able to say she loved him. For years he had always been around and involved in her life (step five). The only mistake he made was in not initiating step seven sooner.

Major Dobbins is also a perfect example of everything I write about the pleasures of love, for it was said of him: "*He never said a word to Amelia that was not kind and gentle; or thought of a want of hers that he did not try to gratify.*" Should you love someone and desire to prove that love, you must do many things to please him. You should love people who treat you as Major Dobbins treated Amelia, even in the absence of that emotion-called-love. Amelia eventually woke up to the fact that Major Dobbins was necessary to her happiness; that his behavior pleased her very much. She finally realized she loved him. We should remind ourselves to be more aware of other people in our lives, more aware than Amelia was of Major Dobbins, so no time is wasted in enjoying a good relationship.

If you have someone who is faithful and good to you now, you may want to evaluate his importance rather than taking him for granted. Losing such a person because you failed to appreciate his true goodness would be a sad mistake. Sweethearts are rare and very hard to find.

Six Weeks to Love

Now, what's this about six weeks being the average time to fall in love? I estimate six weeks because of what happened when I was in basic training in the United States Army. On Monday morning of the sixth week of basic training, one of our sergeants called a formation and presented the following speech: "All right, you guys," he said. "You'd better pay attention to what I have to say, and you'd better pay attention good. This is 'Dear John Week.' Some of you guys are going to be getting a letter from your wives and sweethearts back home saying that they're through with you. I'm sorry about that, but let me tell you this. You'd better not go AWOL over it or I'll come and get you. Do you understand?"

You know, he was right. That very day one of the men in my barracks received a letter from his wife of two years saying she wanted a divorce. As the weeks went by, several other letters showed up. That's why I say it takes that amount of time to fall in love. According to the U.S. Army, the women back home only need six weeks to find a new relationship.

This story also explains two contradictory riddles of love. Which is true? "Out of sight, out of mind" or "Absence makes the heart grow fonder."

As far as our soldier is concerned, absence made *his* heart grow fonder. Remembering our point system, you should be able to see that the girl back home acquires more and more points from him as time goes on because she symbolizes all that is beautiful and pleasurable in this world. As a consequence, he spends every spare moment, of every day, thinking about her. He writes letter after letter to her and never misses a mail call himself. The girl back home acquires more points now than she had when he was home. Thus, absence makes his heart grow fonder and fonder and fonder.

From her side of the fence, the outlook is different. Although she may be in love with him, she still has needs that are clamoring to be satisfied. Thus, she guiltily begins to date others. The end result is a new boyfriend gets points and her soldier loses them. Finally, after about six weeks, the soldier has few points left. Why? Well, she hasn't thought about him for weeks now and, in fact, she hasn't even opened the letters she received last week. She doesn't miss him like she used to because she has been busy with her new boyfriend. Oh well! As they say, "Out of sight, out of mind."

It doesn't always work this way, of course. She could be sitting at home day after day, night after night, moping and sulking and driving her friends crazy; while he, the dirty rat, is having a jolly old time, getting drunk and chasing wild women every weekend.

Women begin by resisting a man's advances and end by blocking his retreat.

Oscar Wilde

CHAPTER 13

Threats to Love Relationships: The "I Love You" Trigger

"Jealousy is not a barometer by which the depth of love may be read. It merely records the degree of the lover's insecurity. It is a negative, miserable state of feeling having its origin in a sense of insecurity and inferiority."

~ Margaret Mead

TIME DEPENDENCY IS NOT UNIQUE TO LOVE RELATIONSHIPS. THE truth is, one can depend on all sorts of people and situations for survival. The brain keeps track of all those needs and responds with emotion any time one is lost. Since it does so by constantly monitoring time, you could stretch my idea to include all people and things we come to depend upon. Should you get fired from a job you desperately need, for example, the emotion that is produced by the brain to fight the threat is usually anxiety or worry. In love relationships we call the *same* internal changes love or heartbreak. The situations simply change the name of the emotion.

Still, the brain's response and the resulting physiological changes are the same under all circumstances involving threats to survival.

Threats

How you initiate step seven is important. The more severe the threat, the more intense the resulting emotion will be. The more severe the emotion, the more the lover feels he is in love—up to a point. Emotion that is too intense is intolerable. As a result, the emotion could be interpreted as hate instead of love, for the negative emotions connected with love and hate feel (and are) the same inside the body.

The word *threat* in this context sounds harsh. Actually, it doesn't have to be an aggressive action. You may have noticed I used the word *disappointment* to introduce step seven. The idea was that the emotion would develop because of some disappointment experienced in the relationship. I switched to the word *threat* because the object is to disrupt, or threaten to disrupt, the habits that were established as a result of time dependency. This can be accomplished in thousands of ways.

Should you desire to create an intense emotion in your lover's body, you aim at the strongest and most consistent habits. For example, if you have been going to lunch with your lover for months on end without missing once, that habit has a great deal of *habit strength.* Consequently, not showing up some day when you were expected will create an emotion in your lover's body that could be severe—especially if he thought you didn't want to show up. *The intensity of the emotion your lover feels is under your control.* And, unfortunately for you, vice versa.

I know of a case where a young man managed to get his girlfriend to tell him she loved him (for the first time) within ten seconds of his prediction, which he made several months earlier. He was able to do so because he followed the seven-step formula perfectly *and* our society believes that love is an emotion.

Considering these facts, it makes sense for lovers not to purposely threaten their relationships—ever. Why not? I have several reasons. First, the emotion feels bad. In fact, it feels terrible. If the relationship has progressed to any degree, some fondness or affection should be felt between the two people. Using an old cliché: if you care for your lover, you won't want him to feel bad. So, don't purposely threaten the relationship.

Since you know how the formula for love works, you should be more cautious and considerate of your lover's feelings. Intentionally threatening the relationship is unnecessary anyway because all that is really necessary is to maintain time dependency and step seven will eventually take care of itself due to environmental threats.

Environmental Threats

Environmental threats are ones the lovers have no control over. They eventually arise in all relationships and will cause the emotion to occur. Example: remember the lady in a previous chapter who was unsure whether or not she was in love with Tom? Suppose that immediately after her phone conversation ended, the phone rang. It is Tom's mother, and Tom has just been in an automobile accident and is in the hospital in serious condition. Would you expect that at the *instant* she hears this news, she will experience an intense emotion, one she can only interpret as love? She is instantaneously in love. An environmental threat has occurred.

Environmental threats don't need to be as serious as this example. Smaller ones will occur, ones that won't cause such an extreme emotion. Tom could have failed to call her some night when she expected him to phone, not because he didn't want to or didn't try, but because he ran out of gas and couldn't get to a phone (a likely story). While she is waiting for him to phone, a funny feeling slowly begins to creep into her body. Although this feeling may not be dramatic, it still causes her to think seriously about Tom. Does she love him? Is this what love *feels* like?

It is fascinating that she might even begin to imagine what it would be like should Tom ever get killed in an automobile wreck. Remember, things perceived in the imagination are believed by the primitive area of the brain to be real. Her thoughts will increase those funny feelings to unbelievable heights. From then on, even though she may deny being in love with Tom, in her heart she knows she is in love.

Time dependency has struck again.

Casual Threats

There is a group of threats I refer to as *casual* threats. The casual threat is sometimes done on purpose, but is done so nonchalantly that the lover won't realize it was done on purpose. More often than not, however, mistakes in one's conversation cause the threat. These threats can slip into any ordinary conversation, either accidentally or on purpose.

> Generally, threats to love relationships are everywhere.

See if you can determine which of Tom's words will cause his girlfriend to feel threatened. He is talking with her about his job: "It really is a good job and it has a great future for me. Yesterday my boss told me he was very happy with my work and that I can expect a promotion soon that will mean three hundred dollars more a month plus an expense account. Of course, if I get it, I'll have to move to Denver."

Quiz time! Which three words in the above paragraph will cause the emotion to appear? (If you miss the answer, you had better go back and read from the beginning again.) When Tom said, "move to Denver," the only thing she wondered is "what about *us*?"

Generally, threats to love relationships are everywhere. Seeing your lover innocently talking with a member of the opposite sex can cause the emotion to appear. The emotion is automatic if there is any possibility, however remote, that there is any interest in this other person. Then there are accidents, illnesses, and other people's comments. It's frustrating, but whenever you are too time dependent on someone, it is inevitable for you to regularly experience little shots of adrenaline that feel awful and upsetting.

Physical Dependency Threatened

Other circumstances can have an effect upon the intensity of the emotion (other than threats to time dependency), and one of the most obvious is physical dependency. If you are physically dependent upon someone, then he is supplying your bodily needs. He may furnish your food, shelter, clothing, etc. If a person who is both time dependent and physically dependent is threatened, the emotion may be more extreme than if he were only time dependent. However, I think it only appropriate to again state that no matter what emotion the person settles on as a *name* for the internal upheaval (fear, anger, love, anxiety, and a host of other possibilities) the physiological symptoms are always the same.

Mathematically, the intensity of the emotion can vary on a scale according to all the possible combinations of those two factors (since time dependency and the level of the threat determine it). If there is very little time dependency and very little threat, the resulting emotion will be of low intensity (if it occurs at all). Likewise, it may only take a minor threat to cause an emotion that is fairly severe in someone who is very time dependent on another. However, it must be remembered that in all possible combinations, time dependency is the more important factor when comparing the two. A threat that may result in an emotion in a time-dependent person can actually cause anger or dislike in someone who is not time dependent.

Consider this statement—made during a date between two people. First apply it to a time-dependent relationship and then to a couple on their second date. The statement goes something like this: "Well, Susan. I don't quite know how to say this to you, but I'm afraid this is going to have to be the last time we go out together." In a time-dependent relationship, this threat will most likely result in negative emotion, leading to tears and other "normal" physical reactions. If this remark were to be made on a second date, presumably before time dependency was established, the reaction should be less severe. Although, it's possible Susan will take offense and say, "Well! I'm sure that's all right with me. I couldn't care less. Who do you think you are? God's gift to women or something? I'm sure I'll be able to survive without you."

My point: be careful when you initiate step seven; you may get more of a reaction than you bargained for.

The only reason I'm not running for president is I'm afraid no woman would come forth and say she slept with me.
Gary Shandling

Chapter 14

Falling Out of Love: When Love Gets Sticky

"Love's a malady without a cure."

~ Dryden, Palamon and Arcite

CONTRARY TO WHAT DRYDEN SAYS, LOVE DOES HAVE A CURE. ONE can fall out of love in two ways. There's the quick emotional method or there's the long and frustrating method. Both have their advantages and disadvantages. Which one you choose is determined by your circumstances and goals; though sometimes it's your lover who chooses for you.

The first method is perhaps the most common. It is simple enough: one partner tells the other to get lost. The method works well if he doesn't mind getting lost, but it can prove disastrous if he does mind. Usually excessive emotion on the part of the person being dumped is a result of this method. This excessive emotion can lead to extreme behavior. The jilted person may expend an enormous amount of energy in an attempt to talk his lover out of her decision. Tricks may be employed. For example, a man may become totally blitzed on alcohol with the idea that once his lover sees how miserable he is without her, she will repent and promise undying love forever and ever. Since adrenaline is a stimulant and alcohol a depressant, it might make sense to get drunk. For a while at least, one might feel better. One drug counteracts the other. Usually however, getting drunk would be classified as maladaptive behavior that should be avoided.

A further difficulty with this popular get-lost technique is the emotional state of the jilted lover tends to remain with him constantly, which increases the relative time dependency that was part of the initial relationship. The emotion, in essence, forces the jilted lover to think more about his lost love, resulting in the lost lover actually acquiring more points. Thus, *the jilted person becomes even more time dependent than before.*

It's truly exasperating to watch this phenomenon occur. I have personally seen it happen hundreds of times: men and women alike who, although appearing to be only half interested in the person they were dating, absolutely lose their minds when they were dumped. From that point on, they spend an enormous amount of time and energy trying to patch up their mediocre relationships. Why?

> This excessive emotion can lead to extreme behavior.

Because they think they are in love. The "dumping" caused the emotion to suddenly appear and now the person being dumped finds himself in somewhat of a fix. You see, he now feels terrible and the only person who can make him feel better is the person who ended the relationship. No one else can do anything to quash the emotion.

The conclusion of those being dumped is that if they ever hope to feel normal and sane again, they had better get back together with their former lovers today *not tomorrow*.

Does falling out of love have to be so miserable and emotional? Not really, although any time you are faced with the loss of someone you don't want to lose, it is going to be hard. What you have to do is reverse the point system and spend less time together and more time with others. As you become less time dependent, the emotion becomes less powerful. Sounds easy, but it's not!

I'll bet that 90 percent of the time only one person in a couple actually wants to break up. Thus, while they may be spending less time together, the reluctant lover begins to think about his lost love more and more. If you happen to be the dumper, unless you can get rid of points, the old reversal trick won't work; and as long as your lover spends time thinking about you, you are still acquiring points—possibly even more points than before.

This reversal method works best in relationships wherein both people want to break up and both agree that they should do so. The challenge for both of them is to make sure they keep themselves busy with their jobs, their favorite sports, and especially with other people. A new lover helps too, of course.

In many breakups that's exactly what people do. They break off relationships only *after* they have found someone new. With this more considerate technique, a couple can logically agree to become time independent of each other s-l-o-w-l-y so that the emotion is absent throughout the time it takes them to get used to seeing each other less often. This is the friendly way to end a relationship—slowly but surely—for each other's sake. It is one of the ways that former lovers can help guarantee they will always be friends.

However, avoiding the potential emotion still isn't going to be easy. It will take time before you stop thinking about your former love. But patience and new friends will prevail and eventually the emotion will cease to exist.

I can't emphasize enough how important it is to become involved with other people whenever you can. For even though Napoleon maintained that, "The only victory over love is flight," flight will not be enough. Other people cure the emotion-called-love—not flight from it (assuming those other people become the satisfiers of your needs).

For example, if a man does not replace his lover with another, he could theoretically love her forever, even if she is thousands of miles away. Thoughts about her will go through his mind and she will still be earning points. Unless his mind is occupied with something or someone else, he will undoubtedly be thinking about her—year after year after year.

Those of us who have been passionately in love with someone in the past frequently reflect back to those days and wonder what it was we saw in our former lovers. The gorgeous, beautiful, wonderful person we loved can appear to be plain and uninteresting from current standards. Looking back, we understand why poets maintain: "Love is blind."

The Sexual Part of Love

One of the sad aspects of long-term relationships is that the ardent sexual, lustful feelings we have for each other slowly fade with time. After several years of lovemaking, the urgency of sex with a particular person begins to disappear. This is problematic in long-term relationships. A lack of sexual desire in one of the partners leads to a decrease in the amount of sexual activity in the relationship, which often leads to frustration and anger from the other partner.

We can speculate as to why nature designed us this way. Perhaps humans aren't meant to be in long-term relationships. Many researchers maintain that humans, by nature, are the same as other mammals in that our sexual contacts would be numerous if given a free choice.

Renowned biologist and Pulitzer Prize winner Edward O. Wilson states in his groundbreaking book, *On Human Nature*, "If a man were given total freedom to act, he could theoretically inseminate thousands of women in his lifetime."

Perhaps nature's goal is to limit the number of children a woman bears in her lifetime, or perhaps on a more practical level, it's simply a way to encourage everyone to spend time doing other things. If sexual desire didn't fade, we might accomplish nothing else.

Science is trying to help solve fading sexual desire by giving us drugs like Viagra to help couples maintain their sex lives. Maybe the reason we try to maintain such a life is that without such pleasures it's often tough for men and women to put up with each other since they are so different. Previous remarks about the role of oxytocin in love relationships appear to support this conclusion.

The word *romance* suggests a sexual involvement between two people, and in nearly all romances some degree of sexual contact occurs. Even if a couple only goes so far as to hold hands, that physical connection can be sexual in nature. People can get immense pleasure from holding hands with someone. In truth, *the need for sexual contact could be the main reason why people fall in love in the first place.*

Considering this fact, it is obvious that falling out of love with a person who is satisfying your sexual needs is quite difficult. If a romance has developed to the point of extensive sexual contact, when you end the relationship you will think about that individual whenever you think about sex.

Thus, one of the problems with falling out of love involves the difficulty of finding someone new to satisfy your sexual needs. Remember, until you replace your lover in all areas of life, you will continue to feel a loss. The frustration and loneliness associated with sleeping alone at night can serve to prolong the time it takes to fall out of love, even if there might have been very little intimate sexual activity in the relationship. The ten or twenty-year habit of cuddling up with someone under a warm blanket is a tough habit to get over. Add to that the all too common problem that during those twenty years we may have lost a great deal of our personal sex appeal. Other people may like us but they just aren't sexually attracted to us. Thus, we realize that we might be facing a future of sleeping alone for the rest of our lives. That realization can serve to create an even more intense feeling of depression over the breakup.

The Ex-Lover Trap

Beware of the "sympathy for the ex-lover trap." Here is how it can work against you. Once a romance has ended, people feel sorry for the ex-lovers. The sorrow can be aimed at both ex-lovers, though usually it is just aimed at one. Although sympathy sounds okay, it can prolong the time necessary for the ex-lovers to get over each other.

This sympathy actually evidences itself in behavior as attention (reinforcement). Whenever reinforcement occurs, it has the affect of increasing the behavior that was occurring when the attention began. In the ex-lovers' case, this behavior is often sulking, pouting, and crying. As a result, the ex-lovers find themselves sitting at home alone for weeks on end in a self-imposed exile because people feel sorry for them.

Sound crazy? The example is similar to when you were a child and hurt yourself. The pain caused you to whimper a bit, but that's all. However, when your sympathetic mother saw you had fallen down, she rushed to your side, saying, "Oh, you poor dear! Are you hurt? Here! Let Mommy kiss it." This sympathy had the affect of increasing the whimpering to a point of full-throttle crying.

It is possible that some of you who are reading this book are caught in the ex-lover trap. If so, you need to decide which you need most—people's well intentioned sympathy or your own happiness. Force yourself out of the trap by becoming involved with others and ignore the sympathy.

Judgment of beauty can err, what with the wine and the dark.
Ovid

Ovid lived over two thousand years ago—nothing much has changed, I guess.

CHAPTER 15

When Love Backfires: The Struggle For Control

"Often the pretender begins to love truly and ends up becoming what he feigns to be."

~ Ovid

WHEN I'VE DISCUSSED THE CONCEPTS IN THIS BOOK, PEOPLE can generally be divided into two groups based on their responses. Members of group one decide they are never going to allow themselves to become time dependent on another person again. These people have usually been in love before, sometimes several times. Subconsciously they already knew these concepts, but couldn't put them into words. (If you are a member of this group, remember it is the emotion connected to a love relationship—not love itself—that can cause problems.) *Intimate relationships with other people are still desirable—only the degree of time dependency needs to be controlled.*

To some degree, time dependency is inevitable. Unless you are forever isolated from society, you will undoubtedly become time dependent on someone.

Totally avoiding time-dependent relationships isn't the goal anyway. *Being willing and able to deal with the emotional risks involved is the main objective.* By understanding what the

123

emotion really is and why it appears, you can more readily handle the inevitable pain.

Group two consists of people who have never been in love before and who can't wait to use the formula in order to get someone to fall in love with them. If you are a member of this group, this chapter is for you.

> Love can be a power struggle between two people in which one person is always the stronger and the other the weaker.

If you rush headlong into the seven-step formula for love and snare yourself an unsuspecting lover, you must still be careful about what you are doing. Unless you watch yourself closely, you may find that the formula back-fires and blows up in your face, leaving you in a state of shock and wondering where you went wrong.

Realize also, that while using the formula to acquire a lover works, it carries certain responsibilities with it. After all, you are interfering with another person's life, and you should be prepared to make sacrifices for him in return.

My own attitude about the *obligations* each of us has whenever we pursue a new relationship eventually caused me to stop coaching people in the use of the formula. A few of my "successful" students gained power using the formula, and then proceeded to abuse their power.

Love can be a power struggle between two people in which one person is always the stronger and the other the weaker. The weaker loves the stronger more than the stronger loves the weaker—that's why they are weaker. Some people maintain that this power struggle is inevitable. Lovers play the dangerous game entitled (sing it everyone) "You-care-more-than-me-e. You-care-more-than-me-e. So Ha! Ha! Ha!" Some people even go so far as to say the power can never be divided equally between the two or they will always be fighting. Since you don't want to find yourself on the losing end of this power struggle, you had better pay attention now.

Power is attained through the acquisition of points—the more points you acquire, the more power you have in the relationship. Thus, as you are developing a relationship, you want to garner more points from your partner than what you give. How do you accomplish this?

Theoretically, when the two of you are together, both of you acquire the same number of points; however, if one of you is thinking about someone/something else, then the point gain won't be even. Typically, it is when you are away from each other that you can gain more points than you give. In order to do this, you must do two things: keep yourself busy so you don't constantly think about your lover—which gives points away; and don't cancel activities with your other friends. Keep friends an active part of your life.

Inasmuch as you succeed in doing these two things, you should find yourself on top in the power struggle, unless, of course, your lover is doing the same thing in his life, then you'll be even!

Love backfires when your lover has more points than you have, and then, when the relationship is threatened, he doesn't get as upset as you. Truthfully, more often than not, in a newly established time-dependent relationship, power immediately goes to the first lover to throw a wrench at the relationship habits by threatening them somehow. It is often a matter of simple timing.

The use of this power can be treacherous. The person in power can do and say unkind things because he is in control of the relationship. Obviously, I don't recommend this. In fact, don't get involved in a power struggle at all if you can help it.

If you are presently involved in this sort of struggle with your lover, consider this: The you-care-more-than-me game, if played seriously, can destroy the relationship. It can also have the affect of leaving the two of you forever hating each other. *No one wins in this game!*

The struggle for power causes emotion to dominate the relationship; and since emotion is a bad feeling, no good can come from playing the game. Instead, sit down with your lover and discuss the power struggle openly. Analyze each of your positions in the relationship, especially as they relate to time dependency. If one of you is more time dependent than the other, figure out how this dependency can be decreased. Then, quit playing the game. You need each other to some degree or you wouldn't be involved in the first place.

Remember this also: for neuropsychological reasons, time dependency will always cause an emotion when its status is threatened, no matter who you are or how much you know. The difference between people is that some learn to control the emotion rather than let it control them. Should you fall in love with this type of person, all the points and power you have will do you no good. Some people are obstinate and will not allow themselves to be controlled by the emotion. Those people are rare, it's true, but they do exist.

I went out with this one guy. I was very excited about it. He took me out to dinner, he made me laugh—he made me pay. He's like, "Oh, I'm sorry. I forgot my wallet." "Really? I forgot my vagina."
Lisa Sundstedt

CHAPTER 16

Energy Reactions: Softening the Blow

". . . in biology, nothing makes sense except in the light of evolution."
~ Theodosius Dobshansky,
Genetics of the Evolutionary Process

". . . in psychology, nothing makes sense except in the light of biology."
~ Larry K. Mickelson

ONE OF THE MANY QUESTIONS THAT HAS EMERGED AS A RESULT of the formula for love centers around the perplexing question of why the human body reacts as it does when a time-dependent relationship is threatened. In contemplating the formula, most people tend to agree it does indeed work but, in trying to figure out why it works, they draw a blank.

We have already established the formula works because it leads an unsuspecting person into the trap of time dependency. Thus, it seems the real question to be answered is why does time dependency cause the body to react emotionally when it is threatened? What function does the emotion serve? Even more pertinent: what is an emotion in the first place?

Fred Enters The Picture

Early in my high-school teaching career, I had an experience that forever changed my perceptions about the nature and purpose of human emotions.

One evening, I was working on some paperwork when Fred, an eighteen year-old student, slipped into my classroom. I almost didn't notice him because he said nothing. He simply came in and sat down in the desk directly in front of my desk. After I greeted him and asked what I could do for him, he just stared at me. It looked like he had been crying, but I wasn't sure.

I could tell Fred was upset about something because he began to tightly clutch the desktop. I naturally assumed he was having girl troubles. After several minutes and much coaxing from me, he finally attempted to talk. His words, however, wouldn't come out.

Because of his difficulty speaking, I figured whatever was bothering Fred was serious. It took several minutes and much tribulation before he was finally able to mutter something about his dad. I knew then that his problem was potentially serious and not something minor like being dumped by a girlfriend (as if girl problems are ever minor).

After at least thirty minutes of this emotional roadblock, I still knew nothing more than when we had started. Fred's every attempt to talk failed. He couldn't say more than a few words before he would begin to tremble and lapse into tears. He tried to leave the room several times because he was so embarrassed. Of course, I couldn't let him leave, so the time dragged on.

I'm not exactly sure what prompted me to come up with the idea, but at some point I told him to go outside and run around the school as fast as he could. Fred was an athlete so I figured it wouldn't hurt him to do so. After he left, I walked over to the window and watched him as he ran past. He was really moving!

When Fred came back in, he sat down and, of course, he was sweating and breathing heavily. Yet, between his puffing and panting, he spoke to me clearly and distinctly. His original speech went something like this. "Mr. Mick, I need to talk to you about my dad. We are not getting along lately and he has been beating me up whenever I see him. I'm afraid to go home after school because he'll be there."

Fred was a nice kid; yet his father found fault in everything he did. His childhood had been fraught with similar incidents. During my subsequent inquiries, I learned that when Fred was very young his father used to tie him to a tree in the front yard of their house for hours on end.

Our first meeting lasted several hours and before it was over Fred had run around the building several more times. Each time he would start to stutter, around he would go.

One of the most valuable lessons both of us learned that day was *exercise seemed to eliminate the unpleasant feelings associated with his emotional state*. Fred was ecstatic with this realization because he was then able to take control over his emotional fear of his father. From that day forward, whenever he began to feel nervous about going home, he would simply go outside and run around for a while.

Once he began to utilize exercise to calm down, Fred was also able to behave more rationally whenever he was around his father. We agreed that first day that perhaps some of the conflicts were being caused by his emotional reactions to things his father said to him.

After our discovery, Fred was better able to control his need to fight back whenever problems developed between he and his dad. He was able to simply listen to his father's tirades without talking back and provoking him further. This is not to say that he didn't have a few more run-ins with his dad, because he did. However, they were shorter and milder in nature. He managed to get through his senior year and then he was off to college in a town far, far away.

Analysis

Did it surprise you that Fred was able to talk with me so clearly after running around the school? I was totally fascinated and the observation has affected me ever since. From that point on, I have thought hard about why it happened. Eventually, I began to reach some conclusions.

In this book, I have stated that the human body will automatically and instantly produce enough energy to deal with any threat it perceives. Fred simply had too much energy inside his body because his father was threatening him physically. By running around the building, Fred burned up that extra energy, allowing his body to return to homeostasis (normalcy). Thus, he was able to talk.

After my experience with Fred, it wasn't long before I came up with this definition of *emotion*:

A (NEGATIVE) EMOTION IS AN INSTANTANEOUS REACTION TO REAL OR IMAGINED THREATS RESULTING IN AN INCREASED ENERGY POTENTIAL OF THE BODY FOR THE PURPOSE OF FIGHT OR FLIGHT.

The internal biological changes one experiences when a time-dependent relationship is threatened are the same sort of reactions that occur when one is attacked by a lion. The body prepares itself for the threat by instantly producing extra energy for the purpose of either fighting or running. Under these and similar circumstances, the body goes on what could be called a "red alert." Any sort of danger, including *anticipated or imagined* dangers, causes this reaction. Whether the danger is in the form of an attacking lion, an approaching tornado, an abusive parent, a bill collector or a rival to one's lover, the reaction is always similar. In all cases, *the intensity of the red-alert status is directly correlated to the perceived seriousness of the danger.*

From a biological perspective, literally hundreds of physical changes can take place inside the body in its attempt to either produce more energy or to conserve energy for future use. The body's internal changes range from the commonly known ones like increases in heart rate and blood pressure, to some rather peculiar ones, like an increase in the production of white blood cells and a decrease in digestion. How many of these changes take place in any given situation is determined by how serious the threat really is *and* its duration.

The more serious the perceived threat, the more changes there are; and the more persistent the threat, the more subtle they become.

There are so many permutations and combinations of symptoms it is difficult, if not impossible, to categorize them in any fashion. There are undoubtedly dozens of biological changes that can take place depending upon the level of the perceived threat. Consequently—and this is of extreme importance—any attempt to separately classify various emotions and their biological symptoms is foolish. Some researchers maintain that the symptoms of fear will be different from the symptoms of, let's say, anxiety. Yet, if you'll recall from previous discussions, it is my contention that the person experiencing the symptoms randomly applies the emotional *name* to the symptoms. Thus, it would seem that attaching a bunch of symptoms to a particular emotion is a mission impossible.

A New Perspective

What do I suggest instead? It isn't that difficult to classify all of the instantaneous energy reactions as being simply "energy reactions." When these reactions occur inside our bodies, we can surmise that, for some reason, the primitive area of our brains has concluded that we need a quick shot of extra energy. We can further conclude the brain has also determined that our survival has been threatened, which is exactly why the energy is suddenly available.

Suppose you are happily working at your job when a fellow worker comes up to you and states that the boss wants to see you in his office *immediately*. The instant you hear this, your body produces energy to prepare for some sort of danger. Later, you might tell friends that when you heard the news it upset you or worried you or scared you because you couldn't imagine what your boss could possibly want. You might be afraid you are about to be fired. As you walk toward his office you can feel your heart beating inside your chest and your hands begin to shake. A slight bead of perspiration begins to show on your forehead.

You have experienced an emotional reaction of some sort; whatever name you decide to attach to those feelings is up to you. We have already used four words to describe your feelings: *upset, worried, scared,* and *afraid.* While walking to your boss's office, you might also feel *irritated* and even *angry* at him (six words and counting). During the trip, your mind jumps forward in time and tries to figure out how you are going to live if you do get fired. The thought *depresses* you and a feeling of *anxiety* pervades your thoughts (eight).

By the time you enter his office you have decided that if he criticizes your work you are going to tell him you quit—before he can fire you. You can hardly control yourself and your voice shakes when you greet him. Time seems to be going in slow motion. After a brief conversation he gives you a raise and thanks you for being such a fine employee. You breathe a sigh of relief and gleefully head back to your desk.

A great story, don't you think? But, what is my point?

Can you see how much simpler it is to realize that something caused your brain to think your survival was threatened, which caused an energy reaction? That is all that has happened.

So, let's review the same story from this new perspective. You are working happily when the fellow worker informs you the boss wants to see you in his office immediately. You notice how he emphasized the word "immediately" and you catch your primitive brain focusing on that word—a sure sign of an up-coming criticism—otherwise what's the rush? So—it's the emphasis on urgency that upsets you. You come to that conclu-sion in a split second and you feel the rush of adrenaline racing through your body. Calling a spade a spade means you simply realize you have experienced an energy reaction, which may require exercise to remove it after work.

As you stroll down the hall toward the boss's office, you go through a self-analysis and attempt to determine why you felt so threatened. You realize intellectually that you have most likely jumped to conclusions and flashed embarrassing, poverty-stricken pictures to your imagination. You know the energy reac-tion was produced instantly, without any conscious control available to prevent it and you also know it won't go away until whatever threatening thought caused it is removed. You conclude that perhaps you are too financially dependent upon this job and you determine to look for more ways to earn extra money in the future. Having all of your eggs in one basket is unwise.

Quite a different view wouldn't you say? Incidentally you might also have realized that even if you do get fired, the extra energy was useless anyway. So the best thing to do is to simply take a deep breath and go into his office and find out what he wants. Prepare for the worst but expect the best.

The All-Encompassing Word

Whenever we become emotional, no matter how slight or serious, we are inclined to describe our feelings with the word *upset*. We can be "kind of upset," "very upset" and everything in between. The word has incredible utility when it comes to expressing feelings.

I believe the word *upset* is the best way to describe the internal upheaval and should, therefore, replace all other words that describe negative emotions. When we are jealous, we can just as easily be upset. When angry, *upset* works again. Frightened, irritated, anxious, embarrassed, hurt, depressed, nervous, worried, etc.—all of these can be replaced by the word *upset*.

Thus, the only task might be to figure out how to calm yourself down. Maybe exercising, breathing deeply, or switching your thoughts to some future fun might help.

By doing something to calm yourself, you can begin dealing with the energy itself rather than calling it fear, worry, or any other emotion. *Those feelings inside you aren't worry or anger or anxiety or hatred or fear or anything else. They are simply related to how it feels to have an excessive amount of energy you don't need.* Your energy teeter-totter is out of balance. Too much energy is being produced; not enough is being burned.

Few of us enjoy those upset feelings, and seeing them for what they really are is comforting; comforting because emotional confusion begins to disappear.

Incidentally, if you can pinpoint the *exact* thought that triggered the instantaneous reaction you'll learn a great deal about yourself. Sometimes it's a tough thing to do because it all takes place within a split second. The amygdala, a small almond sized organ in the primitive brain, is responsible for this speedy reaction.

Whenever you feel an instantaneous energy reaction, you can be assured that your primitive brain has concluded you have been threatened (now or in the past)—physically, socially, or psychologically. Whether there is any real truth involved remains to be seen. Frankly, the reaction is wrong more often than not. Remember—the reaction is being controlled by the stupid part of the brain—not the smart part.

Summary

Any time your survival is threatened, your body will react by producing extra energy. As individuals, we feel these changes take place inside our bodies and conclude that we are experiencing emotional reactions. Which emotions we are feeling is determined by the intensity of our internal arousals and by the circumstances that caused them to occur.

In the case of an attacking lion, we are taught to conclude we are experiencing fear. An approaching tornado causes apprehension if the arousal is slight and fear if the arousal is extreme. An incessant bill collector signals worry, and a rival lover creates jealousy. We decide which emotion we experience by determining how we *feel* about the circumstances that caused the arousal. In essence, *the name applied to a particular emotion is a socially determined formula.* In other words, should we experience an energy reaction because a lion is attacking us, we would not call the feeling jealousy.

In connection with the energy reaction caused by time

> We decide which emotion we experience by determining how we feel about the circumstances that caused the arousal.

dependency, it could be said that this increase in the energy level of the body is especially inappropriate. When your lover threatens your relationship in some way, that extra energy only serves to make you feel rotten. In most cases, you can't use the energy to any practical advantage. You can't run from your lover (although some people do) and you can't fight with your lover (although some people do).

Usually, and unfortunately, the most creative souls:

1. Try to convince their lovers to come back to them by harassing and terrorizing them into submission.

2. Attempt to deal with the feelings in other ways (fighting, kicking dogs, punching walls, barking at friends, pouting, etc.)

3. Get drunk. (Getting drunk works because alcohol is a sedative, and as such, it works to counteract the extra energy by making the brain incapable of producing any energy at all.)

Obviously, many other forms of behavior can help you cope with the emotion. How you react to the feelings inside your stomach will be determined by numerous factors, ranging from your physical makeup to your mental attitude. (Based upon what happened to Fred, might it even make sense to run around buildings when one is heartbroken? In fact, it does indeed make sense *and is undoubtedly the best initial choice; aside from eliminating the problem itself.*)

The point is that, in a general sense, negative emotions are primitive reactions to threats that don't generally require extra energy in order to deal with them. I view the reaction as being a *mistake of nature*, a mistake that will continue to haunt man for many more eons. Only rarely is the extra energy that is produced truly functional.

Intellect Versus Emotion

Ideally, man's intellect should completely take over the task of his survival. Our primitive reactions only serve to confuse us and should be ignored whenever possible. This approach flies in the face of current advice telling us to listen to our emotions and feelings—but it seems obvious that listening to the reptilian brain can't be the intelligent thing to do.

Even during crises of survival, where extra energy would seem to be useful, as in combat situations in the armed forces, the calm, clear-thinking, intelligent man would appear to be at an advantage.

Primitive man survived because, prior to the development of his intellect, his body was capable of producing extra energy at a moment's notice, making him more able to avoid other predators. It is ironic that this ability has now become a disability in that emotional man could destroy himself.

The difference between man and animals lies in the fact that man has to learn to survive physically, socially, and psychologically. The problem with man is that his body reacts to all three forms of threat in the same way.

The physiological changes involving the increase in the energy potential of the body are all too often inappropriate and useless. As I have pointed out earlier, such is the case in regard to the emotion-called-love. When one, for example, loses his loved one in a traffic accident, his future survival may indeed be threatened, both physically and socially, but the extra energy that is produced inside the body only serves to make matters worse. The homeostatic imbalance (internal instability) that is created at that time can actually become self-destructive. A person experiencing grief due to the loss of a loved one is not a healthy person, and indeed, unless the body ceases to produce excessive energy, the person may eventually develop physical disorders that can lead to death. Such is the case with most psychosomatic disorders in medicine (illnesses due to emotional instability). *A physical, social, or psychological threat triggers the energy production inside the body that remains there until the threat is removed.*

Just So You'll Know

I have come up with an analogy for how the brain deals with impending dangers, described as a little guy named Fred living deep inside one's brain. Fred sits in a swivel business chair with rollers, while watching six television screens in order to find out what is going on in the world outside of his tightly enclosed room. Numerous buttons and switches used to control the entire body are located in front of him. Should a gauge on the panel indicate, for example, that the bladder is full, Fred can flip a switch (hormones released) and create sudden unpleasant sensations within the body, forcing said body toward necessary bathroom. Success? Switch off.

One valuable piece of equipment available to him is a massive computer full of information about all things good and all things dangerous (survival facts). Some of the information in the computer comes from notes Fred has taken himself since birth (memories whether conscious or unconscious), while other details have been downloaded from a centuries-old database (truths from ancestors—for example, loud noises and fast movement are universally dangerous. All humans automatically respond with energy reactions when they occur). Fortunately, he can scan the entire hard drive in a split second, giving him much valuable information. Should Fred determine that something is showing up on the television screens that could threaten life and limb, he has a large button within reach that he can slap. Of course, this is the red-alert energy button and he isn't shy about using it. His motto is: "Better safe than sorry."

The television screens are representative of the five senses. Thus, whatever the eyes see, he sees on one of the screens, etc. The sixth screen is the screen of imagination.

It is important to remember that Fred *absolutely* believes everything that shows up on any of the screens. Decisions are made without forethought. He simply responds. He is unconcerned with truth—he only wants facts (as they appear on the screens). If he sees some green-eyed, sharp-toothed monster coming at him (in a movie being viewed by his eyes) he is going to hit the alert button and demand that subject body get out of Dodge. Of course, the intelligent part of the brain knows the movie is make-believe, so no running is allowed—override buttons prevent him from controlling the arms and legs. Still, because the red-alert button had actually been pushed, the individual will conclude that the movie was scary (upsetting).

The screen of imagination is especially problematic. My personal Fred recently woke me with a start, because I was riding a bike in my dreams (imagination again) and I almost fell off a cliff. I can still picture the rocks and the view downward. Fred didn't appreciate that view, so he hit the button.

I enjoy tricking Fred because now I know how he operates. I don't appreciate the numerous times he has unnecessarily hit that stupid button; upsetting me for no good reason. Why, for example, does Fred think I need extra energy just because I'm betting money on a golf game? If he would stay out of it, I would do just fine. But no! He gives me extra energy and then I can't seem to putt.

Thus, whenever I'm involved with something that could possibly be upsetting (threatening), I attempt to send Fred a tranquil picture, to deceive him.

Instead of getting married again, I'm going to find a woman I don't like and just give her a house.
Rod Stewart

CHAPTER 17

The Theory of Contrasts: Why Nice Guys Finish Last

"Little quarrels often prove to be but new recruits of love."

~ Butler, Hudubias

I ONLY RECENTLY CAME UP WITH THE OUTLINE FOR THIS BOOK, but once I did, things began to fall into place. The four types of love clear up many of the confusing and contradictory beliefs we have been taught about love. A minor example of such contradictions was discussed in the chapter "Love's Time Schedule." Is it true that "absence makes the heart grow fonder" or is "out of sight out of mind" the better explanation? We have all heard the two dictums, but now we know when each is true. Time dependency clears everything up.

The Fifth "I Love You"

Even so, something else about the "mystery" of love has been bugging me. As it turns out, I found the answer when I recently re-read the first manuscript I wrote many years ago, specifically in a chapter entitled, "Love and the Theory of Contrasts." That chapter contained one of the most significant observations possible about love.

139

So, to introduce this section, I will include an excerpt from the chapter:

> Several years ago, a friend of mine managed to lodge a tiny piece of steel in his eye. His eye turned red, began watering voraciously, and he started blinking uncontrollably. Whenever we looked for anything that might be in his eye, we saw nothing. After several days of this, he began to experience a great deal of pain, until finally he made an emergency appointment with an ophthalmologist, who located and extracted the piece of steel.
>
> When I met my friend about an hour after the appointment, he was ecstatic. In fact, his mood was so good that he was almost unbearable. He ran around as if he had lost his marbles and continuously poked me in the ribs and teased me. He tried to wrestle with everyone we encountered; he talked louder than usual; and, in general, acted very peculiarly. When I accused him of being on joy juice or something similar, he vehemently denied it and claimed that his mood was simply the result of his success at getting the piece of steel out of his eye.
>
> That was easy enough to understand, since I would have felt elated under the same conditions; but something he said later really threw me. During one of his heel-clicking "spasms," he made the remark that he was actually glad the steel had gotten into his eye because he felt so "high" now that it had been removed.
>
> What does this have to do with love? In answering this, let me first remark that this "Theory of Contrasts," as I now call it, is for me one of the most frustrating objections to my system of logic. People who believe and identify with my friend's thinking are the same type who will maintain that a love relationship isn't worth having unless it *hurts* once in a while. They believe you have to experience pain before you can know how great pleasure can be. Now I know that all desirable relationships will eventually have some painful moments caused by uncontrollable threats, but I sure wish it didn't have to be the case.
>
> Okay! Those of you who agree with my friend, answer this for me: if the theory of contrasts is valid and I am a friend to this man, doesn't it seem reasonable that I, as his friend, should punch him in the nose a time or two whenever I see

him so that he, the lucky dog, can feel good when I quit? This seems logical to me based upon our previous conclusions.

I probably should point out to those of you who are on my side of this debate that my friend isn't as rare a breed as one might think. In fact, in some ways, our entire society believes in the theory of contrasts from time to time. Two examples stand out as being representative of this fact. The first one relates perfectly to the topic of this book. There is a belief among the men in this country that if you treat a girl too nicely you'll never get anywhere with her. While women swear that the idea is absurd, at times it seems to be true, and from one perspective it is true.

Consider, for example, what is implied by the seventh step of our formula: a person is supposed to disappoint his lover in some way in order to create the emotion in his lover's body. Yet doing so is no different than if I were to punch my friend in the nose. The idea is still to make your lover feel bad so that she will appreciate you more when you are making her feel good. (The sad part is that it works.) In fact, sometimes, unless you do something to make her feel bad, she never does appreciate you. And without the seventh step of the formula, the emotion-called-love may never make its appearance.

Another good example of the theory of contrasts, and one that used to plague me whenever I lectured on love, calls for a discussion relating to a technique for rating movies. We all know there are good movies and bad movies with ratings ranging from G to X. However, these ratings tell us nothing about the quality of the movie. There is a way, however, that some movies could be rated that would be much more effective in describing the action. Depending upon what happens in the plot, movies could be rated according to whether they are "one-tear movies," "two-tear movies," on up to the ultimate "five-tear thriller." This rating system indicates how many times the soft of heart can expect to cry during the movie.

After a five-tear thriller has been shown in a theater, the janitor could expect to fill the trashcans with soaking-wet Kleenex tissues. These five-tear thrillers are the crème de la crème and can be expected to pack the theaters across the country. People seem to like movies the most that make them cry the most. The entire idea used to confuse me.

Why would someone want to cry? For years, I assumed these tears were merely another example of the theory of contrasts. I finally came to realize, however, that the feelings people experience during these movies should not be called emotions at all. Something entirely different is occurring."

Discussion

Ever since I wrote that chapter I have been mulling it over. My friend's behavior still seems peculiar, but it has led to some extremely important observations about love and human behavior. There is something peculiar about humans if we operate in this fashion. And we do operate this way—*unless the intellectual part of our brain overrides such nonsense.* You don't think so? The fact is that problems in relationships often signal and even classically demonstrate, love. We have seen this with the seven-step formula. Now, I must warn you, we will again see it in this section, but from a more subtle perspective.

In our outline, we concluded there are four times when lovers are inclined to use the phrase "I love you." This section will search out and isolate a fifth. Based upon the theory of contrasts, we have three clues.

1. The euphoria created by the removal of the steel from my friend's eye.

2. The universal belief and observation that nice guys finish last. The question here is what exactly is the bad boy doing to a woman to make him the preferred lover in spite of all logic to the contrary?

3. The phenomenon in movies, books, and stories that causes people to joyfully cry.

If we can make sense of all of these clues, perhaps there is a lesson to be learned, one not only about love but also about life and human behavior in general.

Ah yes, divorce…From the Latin word meaning to rip a man's genitals through his wallet.
Robin Williams

CHAPTER 18

The Concept of Emotings: A New Genre of Feelings

"Ever has it been that love knows not its own depth until the hour of separation."

~ Kahlil Gibran

FOR MANY YEARS, I BELIEVED THERE WERE NO POSITIVE emotions. I concluded that even love, presumably the most positive emotion of all, was a negative one (as per the formula).

In truth, negative emotions are negative only because the individual experiences them in a negative way. (This is not meant to be a riddle.) The problem is excess energy inside the body is disruptive and feels bad. As I have stated, excess energy upsets people—even though initially the energy was beneficial since it helped mankind survive as a species. However, the beneficial attributes of such a system of energy production in today's world is questionable.

I have speculated about what would happen if science could figure out how to tie Fred's hands or to somehow disconnect the red-alert button, thus preventing all the bad feelings. The negative emotions would disappear and, indeed, my seven-step formula would become obsolete.

(Many years ago, I wrote a screenplay for a science fiction

143

love story, *Keystone: A Love Story*, about the success of such an enterprise. The story is an expansion of these concepts. It is available on my website.)

The other, supposedly positive emotions like joy and happiness, I viewed as simply being normalized, quiescent states characterized by *an absence of negative emotion.* A person felt good (normal) rather than bad (emotional) and was therefore able to express intellectual happiness or joy. The theory of contrasts is moderately at work again.

I used to get a kick out of asking people if they were happy. Some would respond in the affirmative but when asked what that felt like, most would draw a blank. One woman's response was illuminating and worth noting. She stated that she was happy but that it didn't feel like anything in particular. She believed happiness was simply the opposite of unhappy and since she was not unhappy then naturally she determined she was happy. She didn't need lights to flash or bells to ring; she simply enjoyed feeling normal and healthy. For this reason and more I had decided that we really had no need for the so-called "positive emotions."

Eventually though, I noticed that if there are positive feelings/emotions in life, most of them appear after something negative has been removed. For example, should a destitute, down-on-his-luck fellow find a fifty-dollar bill blowing down the street, he will undoubtedly express sheer *joy* at his good fortune. He will also likely experience a gleeful, joyous day with a satisfied smile throughout.

From a somewhat obtuse perspective, one could conclude that his joyous feelings were caused by his poverty—since it is apparent that if a multimillionaire were to have found that same fifty, he would have simply picked it up and put it in his pocket without giving much thought to it at all.

How do five-tear movies fit into the puzzle? When we cry, are our tears classified as being a positive emotion? If so, has some sort of negative been removed (like the relief my friend felt when the steel was removed from his eye)?

Since people flock to movies that make them cry, one could

conclude that crying represents a positive experience. But what name is the positive experience to be given? My dilemma in naming the feelings has always been caused by my preference to reserve the word *emotion* for the negative emotions. So, I needed a new word to describe crying that was caused by tearjerkers. People refer to this crying as "getting all choked up" or "being teary-eyed." I wasn't happy with those phrases either.

Finally, the dictionary solved my problem. When I looked up *emotion*, the word *emote*, a verb, caught my eye. While *emote* is just another word for feeling or being emotional, it is seldom used in everyday life. Consequently, I hijacked the word and began using it to describe the crying in movies and elsewhere. Now, instead of asking people how many times they got all choked up in a particular movie, I instead ask how many times they *emoted*. I also turned the word into a noun by referring to it as an *emoting*.

> Emotings are positive feelings and appear on the Survival of the Species side of the outline.

Relative to the entire outline of this book, *emotings* are positive feelings and appear on the Survival of the Species side of the outline. *Emotions* are negative energy reactions that appear on the individual side.

Affection for someone, as described in the chapter on attachment love, implies a close, personal, pleasurable relationship caused by pleasure hormones, while emotings can often occur in connection to someone or something frequently and entirely disconnected personally. We feel affection for those near and dear to us, while we are able to emote about something that happens to strangers on the other side of the earth. Further reading will clear this up.

The Characteristics of Emotings
1. Crying in movie theaters differs from other emotions in that we want to cry while watching these movies.

People flock to theaters around the country just so they can cry a time or two. This is certainly different from most other emotions. How often do we go out of our way, for example, to have our feelings hurt, or to be angry, depressed, embarrassed, etc.?

2. Emotings are similar to emotions in that they occur at *predictable times.* If you think back to the formula for love, you will recall I maintained that the emotion-called-love could be *predicted* to occur at an *exact* moment in time and could be predetermined by the person using the formula. The emotion, then, was both predictable and instantaneous. These two characteristics are oddly important in any discussion about human emotion. There is a *guarantee* that extremely time-dependent people will experience an instantaneous energy reaction whenever faced with the loss of the person they are time dependent upon.

3. Relative to and in comparison to the emotion created in a love relationship, emotings are predictable but *not instantaneous.* They also have nothing to do with the production or conservation of extra energy. Patrons in a theater who are concentrating on the movie are predictably going to experience a "welling up of tears." However, you will note that the welling up of tears develops slowly, over a period of several seconds or minutes. One can feel them coming on. We can sense that we are about to emote and, if for some reason we don't want to, we have to look away from the screen in order to stop the reaction. If the movie is well done and the writing is perfect, tears will flow in all of us—even if we might be "real men."

4. Physiologically, emotings are undoubtedly quite different from emotions. Think about some of the symptoms of classic emotional states. Now I ask you—when you are crying in a movie theater, do you think there is a sudden rush of adrenaline in your body? I doubt it. And I doubt that you display many of the other

classic symptoms either. In fact, the crying appears to have a comforting effect upon you. After a really great tearjerker, any tension or stress you may have felt before watching the movie seems to have lessened or disappeared. You feel more relaxed and peaceful. (That sounds like the work of some of the attachment hormones like oxytocin and/or vasopressin).

5. Thus, people experience emotions and emotings. The difference between the two can be understood by going back into the movie theaters. When we attend horror flicks, for example, we know the director is going to try to scare the daylights out of everyone. The *instant* he succeeds (I repeat—the *instant*), we all experience an energy reaction.

    One of the most simplistic and, therefore, uncreative ways to accomplish this is to have the monster suddenly jump out of the dark and grab someone. If done just right, screams will be heard for miles. At that *instant*, what do you think is happening inside the bodies of the patrons? Of course—adrenaline and all of its evil partners consume the very souls of the viewers. I swear that during *The Exorcist*, my heart rate must have topped out at 250 beats per minute. As a result, I hated the movie, yet I sure encouraged everyone else to go see it. (Why should I be the only one to suffer?)

    Remember earlier in the book, when I stated: "things perceived in the imagination are believed by the brain to be real?" That is exactly what happens in scary movies. The brain thinks the monster is real and not just a projection on a screen. Because the brain has been fooled, it instantaneously produces energy inside the body to fight or run from that horrible beast.

6. Emotings only last for brief periods of time. When a movie causes us to emote, the tears fade as soon as the scene changes. Maybe that's one of the reasons we like to emote—the feelings are temporary. Compare that to an emotion like anxiety that can last for long periods.

7. Finally, and perhaps most importantly, these tears can be made to occur *by formula* just as the emotion-called-love can be created using the seven-step formula. If one simply follows this formula, people can be made to cry on cue. How? What's the formula? Actually there are a number of them, but I'll focus on two of the more popular ones.

The Predictable Nature of Emotings

The first category is called "Misunderstandings Cleared Up." All that is necessary is to create a conflict or misunderstanding between two people and then miraculously clear everything up. In love stories, whenever two people who absolutely adore each other are about to be forever separated by time and geography because of some silly misunderstanding, it has always been the job of the best friend to somehow explain away the supposed problems that were separating the lovers. Then, just before the brokenhearted lover boards a plane for a far-off place, a frantic pursuit ends with hugs and kisses and profound professions of undying love. If done correctly, just as predicted and at precisely the correct moment, tears will flow. Works every time!

Want examples? Well, let's see. How about *Crocodile Dundee*, *Pretty Woman*, *Overboard*, *You've Got Mail*, *What Women Want*, and hundreds of others!

The other category involves success, especially unexpected success. Anyone who succeeds at something can cause all of us to emote at exactly the right time. Consider awards ceremonies! Small emotings occur in the attendees as each name is called because each award represents some sort of success. But, emotings can be free-flowing and expansive when an underdog succeeds against all odds. Consider a student who nearly died in a car wreck, resulting in numerous mental and physical challenges. Add to that the fact that because of his disabilities he lost the girl he loved. As a result, no one thought he would ever graduate. When this gentleman goes up on the stage, the entire crowd will emote—on cue.

This category could also be called "Triumph Over Adversity"

or "Triumph Against All Odds." Movie examples are: *The Titans, The Natural, The Rookie*, and *Major League*. Our desire and need for superheroes (Superman, Batman) who defeat all things evil fit into this category.

Essentially, anytime there is something going on in one's life that is "not so good," the potential for an emoting is present. If we find ourselves unhappy, broke, sick, needing rescuing, misunderstood, picked on, sad, unloved, unappreciated, over-worked, overlooked, lonely, overly tired, unsuccessful, foolish, anxious, depressed, embarrassed, etc., when something happens to alleviate the situation, we emote. What is interesting is that even if we know ahead of time what will happen, we are still inclined to emote.

Sometimes our emotings are brief in duration and go unnoticed. At other times, millions of people will emote for long periods of time, for example, during times of national crises. The date 9/11 comes to mind. During such events, the aggression involved upsets us (frightens, angers, worries) while the subsequent televised rescues (removals) of those affected cause us to emote—in mass.

Many of the greatest books ever written tell stories about unhappy times, misunderstandings, and the eventual resolution of problems. And, just like the movies of today, they initially depict much sadness and misfortune. Those depictions set the reader up for the inevitable emotings—which is exactly what makes the book popular in the first place. One such story is *A Christmas Carol*. When old Mr. Scrooge finally begins to help others, the tears flow for several pages.

Another fabulous movie for depicting emotings is *It's a Wonderful Life* starring James Stewart. At the end of the movie it looked as if George (James Stewart) was sure to be arrested for bank fraud (the "not so good" part of the formula). Suddenly, the entire town of Bedford Falls comes to his rescue and contributes the money to pay off the bank debt. Anyone who doesn't emote during that scene must be dead.

This movie also contains my personal all time favorite love scene.

Ever since he could remember, George had promised himself that he would somehow get out of his hick town and see the world. Throughout the entire movie, each time he was almost able to leave, something would happen to prevent it. The worst problem was that, as the years passed, he had unintentionally fallen in love with Mary, the local librarian. Truthfully, he had been in love with her for years but was afraid to admit it. He saw marriage as a geographical trap because he longed to leave and travel the world.

During one particular scene, he was so drawn to her that he began to tremble. She was very close to him but his desire to travel prevented him from touching her. While he was talking on the phone, she seductively snuggled up to him, nearly touching her cheek to his. They were so close that her womanly fragrance was nearly his undoing. He wanted so much to admit his love for her but he steadfastly resisted the impulse because doing so would forever condemn him to a life in that one-horse town.

While the two of them listened on the phone, sharing the same receiver, it becomes obvious that their thoughts are only on each other and not the phone conversation. When George finally cracks, he grabs for her and after angrily telling her that he doesn't want to get married, he succumbs to his love and begins to hug and kiss her feverishly. She returns his fervor and—and—we all cry like babies. (Whew! My eyes nearly began to water as I typed! A close call for sure.)

Do you see how the formula works? Can you sense how precise it is?

Shakespeare was truly the master at jerking our heartstrings. He would create a problem and then solve it. On several occasions in *Romeo and Juliet* he impishly implies that everything will turn out perfectly for the two lovers. We emote several times with each apparent solution. When he ultimately disappoints us, we are so shocked we are speechless. Truly he was the best.

Togetherness Through Emotings

Emotings as a concept and a predictable reality fascinate me. Whatever happens inside the human body must have social survival value, which is why I position emotings on the Survival of the Species side of the outline. Whenever I try to understand their purpose, function and value, I move away from any thoughts about personal or self-ish satisfaction (even though we enjoy the feelings they provide) and begin to think in terms of a larger social good. For example, emotings cause people to become more charitable and considerate toward others (like the national response to Hurricane Katrina). Even the patriotic feelings we experience when the national anthem is played at sporting events bond citizens together. *People who emote together tend to develop a bond.*

> Emotings can be described as being part of the survival of the species, while emotions are useful for self-preservation but can be harmful to groups because they signal conflicts.

Groups of all sorts are tied together for political, religious, or other causes because *they have emoted together* at some point in time. Many of these groups develop an us-against-the-rest-of-the-world attitude—a some-times dangerous and destructive mind-set. Emotings can be described as being part of the survival of the species and cause us to help each other when in need, while emotions are useful for self-preservation but can be harmful to groups because they signal conflicts.

Thus, we might conclude that emotings bring us together into groups for common goals. Emotions, on the other hand, separate us.

Emotion Defined

As we have already established, an emotion is an instantan-eous reaction to real or imagined threats resulting in an increased energy potential of the body for the purpose of fight or flight. If a feeling, sensation, mood, or other biological change doesn't fit that definition, *it should not be categorized as an emotion*. Can you see why I created the new category called *emotings*? Emotings do not fit the definition; therefore, they are not emotions. Let's review!

What feelings generally fit the category of emotion? How about fear, anxiety, hatred, jealousy, depression, grief, and hundreds of others with fancier names? They are all "energy reactions" with varying levels of intensity.

In comparison, what feelings fit the category of emotings? How about empathy, sympathy, compassion, caring, and concern?

Emotings versus Emotions in Everyday Life

As an example of the difference between emotings and emotions, let's imagine John, beloved husband of Norma, dies in a car wreck. John and Norma have four adult children, all of whom will attend the funeral.

Sarah, the oldest, has been married for fifteen years, has three kids, and lives in France. She hasn't seen her family for several years and phone conversations are a rarity.

Jason and Mark, the middle sons, are successful professionals who live in a city about two hundred miles from their parents' home. They visit their parents several times a year and usually make some form of contact at least once or twice a week. They each have two kids and are happily married.

The youngest child is Elizabeth. Elizabeth has never married and, as a consequence, she sees her parents every day and knows what is going on in their lives. She and her parents often do things together.

Who is going to cry the hardest at the funeral? Norma and Elizabeth, of course! And would you believe this whole business might affect Elizabeth more than it does her mother? Why? Well, let's look at Norma for a moment.

First of all, there is no question that Norma loved her husband very much. She was happily married to John for thirty-five years. But, about ten years ago, Norma earned her real estate license and was having a ball selling houses. Not only that, but last year she was elected to the city council. Consequently, she often arrived home late in the evenings so she wasn't able to spend as much time with John and Liz as she would have liked.

Let's look at Liz's life a little closer. Last year, when Norma started her term on the city council, the decision was made to have Liz move back home so that she could help her father with things around the house. Since then, she and her dad spent endless hours fishing, hiking, playing golf, and generally having fun together. They were bosom buddies.

Now, if time dependency were to be measured, it appears that Liz would turn out to be more time dependent on her dad than her mother was. Thus, if I am correct in my speculation about time dependency, Liz is going to *emotionally* miss her father more than anyone else—even her mother. In fact, she may miss him for many months or even years since nearly every day of every week she will have no one to go fishing or golfing with. That *lack of companionship* constantly reminds her of how wonderful her father was.

Mathematically speaking (because of the point system), the other three children may feel little *true* emotion during the funeral and consequently they may feel weird and guilty about their lack of emotion. Usually the best they can conjure up "emotionally" falls into the category of "emotings." Conversations involving some fun, exciting, or memorable events that involved their father can create emotings for brief moments.

The welling-up of tears is heartfelt but certainly temporary. The temporary nature of these feelings is one of the things that separate them from the emotion connected to time dependency. Once the three children return to their respective cities, they may never again "miss" their father except on an intellectual level. They may talk about their father with deep feelings of respect and love; but seldom will they cry themselves to sleep because their father has died. Elizabeth and her mother may, on the other hand, cry themselves to sleep for quite some time. They will miss him emotionally.

Here is another observation. Norma may cry at only one particular time each day. When? Well, we are measuring time-dependent periods in Norma's life, so the question is when during the day, week, or month was Norma time dependent on her husband? One period of time stands out—when she arrived home from work each night until the time she left for work in the morning. Can you see how each evening after her husband's death, because of her routine, she may begin to miss him so much that tears are inevitable? And she's probably sleeping alone for the first time in thirty-five years. That is going to take some getting used to.

Put your thinking cap on because I've got a great question for you. Suppose Norma hadn't been overly excited about the relationship she had with her husband before he died? Suppose they had grown apart in the last few years. Let's surmise that John had been somewhat peeved about her job and political life. Consequently, they were inclined to have little disagreements all of the time. Now, in spite of their problems, do you think she would miss him as much?

My answer is yes, of course. Remember—the emotion caused by time dependency is only indirectly connected to love. Thus, in spite of these little disagreements, if Norma's relationship with her husband were pleasant enough to give him the necessary "evening points," then the emotion would be the same. If, when she arrived home at night, she just couldn't wait to tell him about her day; and if she was always curious about the things he and Liz had been up to; and if, when they had finally gone to bed each night, the cuddling was as wonderful and fulfilling as it had always been—then Norma has no choice but to suffer *emotionally* after his death.

In order for this not to happen, Norma would have to be thinking about other people or other activities when she was with him each night. That could have been happening too! Norma was about as busy as anyone could be and, as a result, her thoughts each evening might have been more on her job and city politics. Then again, maybe things had gotten so bad that she had begun fantasizing about some other man at work. Maybe, too, she and her husband had stopped touching each other when in bed at night. The sexual part of their love life may have died years ago and nothing happened to change that. Her home may have become just a place to sleep.

Under those circumstances, she might not miss him much at all. She might have become totally time independent of her marriage because of her busy lifestyle. Norma had lived with and loved her husband for thirty-five years but, now that he has died, she just doesn't *feel* as devastated emotionally as even *she would prefer*. She might feel awkward about her lack of feeling. Of course, she will miss him, intellectually at least, but she has caught herself daydreaming about her future life without him and things don't look that bleak. In fact, while she can't tell anyone this, she looks forward to a possible new relationship with the aforementioned gentleman at work.

Emotings, Emotions, and Love

Let's wrap this up with one more question. Does the fact that the other three children didn't suffer too much emotionally mean they didn't love their father? This is where time dependency stands out as an explanation for the emotion-called-love, because most people would agree that they undoubtedly loved their dad very much.

As further proof, did I mention that Sarah had always been daddy's little girl? Yes, indeed! She was daddy's favorite child. It tore him up when she moved to France. It took quite a while for the two of them to readjust afterwards. For years, the long-distance phone bills were ridiculously high. Yet, in the last five years or so little communication had taken place. Since Sarah wasn't time dependent on him, she will experience no emotion. Again, the presence or absence of the emotion doesn't measure love.

Surely daddy's little girl loved him deeply and will, therefore, be just as upset as everyone else about his death. Again, I reiterate, we are not measuring love here. We are measuring the emotion caused by time dependency. Sarah was in no way time dependent on her father so she *cannot* feel the emotion—even if she wants to. She may emote when she thinks about the wonderful relationship she had with her dad but she can't feel a true emotion because her life is not threatened in any way by his death.

Let's follow Sarah back to her happy and busy life in France. There is no doubt in my mind that during the flight home, thoughts about her dad are going to make her cry. However, those tears are emotings, not emotions. They have a cathartic value to her. Crying on the plane *feels good* and doing so helps her accept her father's death. However, once she lands in France and her loving family greets her with open arms, she may rarely think about her father any more than she had been thinking about him in the recent past. Life has changed for Sarah. The rest of her family is just not in the picture anymore. Period! Period! Period!

That's the way it has to be too. After all, for psychological reasons, we have to be able to emotionally forget people who disappear from our lives—no matter what relationship we had with them. Family, friends, lovers, it doesn't matter. To put it bluntly —all people who no longer help us survive in some fashion are eliminated from our emotional lives and are potentially forgotten.

It's all so practical. The brain's job is to keep us alive—*now*. Only those who help us *now* get much credit and respect. (Don't forget, though, that you can fool the brain with your imagination. Only intellectual man can maintain a memory of people we have loved in the past. Emotional man is predictably going to lose all interest.)

It's not true that married men live longer than single men. It only seems longer; and—the reason women outlive men is simple—they don't have to live with women.

Unknown

CHAPTER 19

The Pleasurable Addiction:
Love's Emotings

"You must get your living by loving."
~ Henry David Thoreau

ONE OF THE REASONS I BELIEVE LOVE IS SO CONFUSING IS THAT it is inextricably tied to both emotions and emotings. Like two birds of a feather, they operate predictably—one after the other. Generally, in the scheme of things, emotion shows up first. When two people in love quarrel or have a disagreement, the emotion connected to love rears its ugly head. The lovers feel sad, depressed, and unhappy as a result.

We have already established that those feelings are caused by time dependency threatened. We have also determined that at this moment, people conclude they are in love. But now it gets interesting. The plot doth thicken.

Did you notice the three words—sad, depressed and unhappy —used to describe the energy reactions of the lovers, would be considered as negative? Thus, according to our formula for emotings, the scene is set for the removal of these negative emotions, thus creating a positive emoting.

The irony of the entire process revolves around the fact that with love, the feelings occur within a closed circle. When two

157

people in love quarrel, they are also the only ones who can correct the problem. Thus, if a negative is removed, it is generally removed by one of the lovers—meaning that the positive emotings that follow will naturally be credited to the other person.

And so it goes. We quarrel—we feel sad—we make up—we emote. When we emote, we become *convinced* we are totally and completely in love. Every fiber of our being points to this conclusion.

Can you sense how the chapter about love and the theory of contrasts was applied here? Remember the fellow who was happy about having gotten a piece of steel in his eye because he felt so great when it was removed? Well, here we go again! It would appear that the exact same thing happens in love relationships. After the quarrel, the making up, and the fantastic sex that follows, lovers are inclined to conclude that quarreling has its good points.

This phenomenon also explains why nice guys finish last. The qualities that make them nice guys work against them because they don't *upset* their girlfriends often enough, so they aren't responsible for emotions or emotings. In contrast, the bad boys of the world are constantly disrupting relationships with all sorts of inconsiderate remarks and disappointing behaviors (once, of course, time dependency has been established), causing the emotional drama and the crying and lamenting peculiar to mediocre relationships. The beloved emotings are close behind.

Incidentally, bad boys are also more inclined to be more sexually aggressive, flattering and demanding towards their lovers. One minute they are telling their women how beautiful and sexy they are and the very next minute they do or say something upsetting or mean or generally inconsiderate. The relationship becomes one huge emotional roller coaster with Mr. Bad Boy calling the shots.

I am currently witnessing just such a relationship. The girl involved is a sweet, beautiful, sexy woman who could have 90 percent of the men in the world (the others would be gay), but she foolishly sticks to a guy who treats her like dirt. It's sad to watch. She looks to be more sad than happy. And while she may realize her relationship isn't the best, she still believes she is in love. I wish I could talk with her but that doesn't seem possible since we are merely acquaintances. I can only hope that someday she will learn to ignore her feelings and then go out and find a nice guy to have a relationship with—one who will love her and respect her for the sweet person she is.

I can't help pointing out that the bad boy syndrome does, of course, work in reverse also. There are many "bad girls" out there constantly jerking the heartstrings of their lovers. They can be just as controlling, inconsiderate, and ruthless as their male counterparts. The men being controlled can also be as foolish and pitiful as the aforementioned women.

Lovers' Quarrels

Two people involved in a shaky relationship argue about something that turns into a major misunderstanding involving many loud unkind exchanges. Both of them retreat to private areas in an attempt to stop the battle.

The air is filled with tension for several days while they stew over the unhappy circumstances. They both begin to fear this problem may end their relationship for good. That prospect frightens them (after all, where would each of them live? And what about the bills? Who is going to pay them?), so they both begin to feel badly about their behavior. Finally, one of them cautiously apologizes.

When the tension in the room gets so thick they both feel like crying, they finally succumb to the pressure of the moment and rush headlong into each other's arms. They hug and kiss and cry volumes of "relief" tears. They say they are sorry and promise to love each other forever. The tears turn to tears of joy and they begin to frantically and passionately make love—which turns out to be the most exciting sex they have ever shared. Profound expressions of love are tearfully exchanged and they express feelings of total bliss.

Love conquers all. Lovers will sell their souls just to experience an emoting in a relationship and the second they do, with all of their hearts and with tears in their eyes they will gush "I love you!!!"

(Incidentally, in order for an emoting to occur, the quarrel part of this story isn't necessary. All that is necessary is for there to be something going on in their lives that is "not so good." It could be the end of a forced separation, a simple misunderstanding cleared up, a sick child cured, or anything similar.)

Ultimately, emotings are caused whenever *anything negative in life is removed*. Use your imagination and the formula and devise your own emoting-creating situations.

Enter the Doubting Thomas

Now, I must ask you again. Is there any doubt the emotings that appear after a lovers' quarrel signal true love? Who would ever doubt that? *Unfortunately for our beliefs about love, I doubt it. I truly do.*

I am aware that I am getting into some murky water here and it's tempting to back off. However, if my ultimate goal is to promote deep thought in readers, I'll simply have to continue.

So, what is it that I doubt? Certainly I don't doubt that our couple thinks they are in love with each other. I don't doubt much loving behavior has taken place between them. I don't doubt both people are happy and content after their experience. Finally, I don't doubt their passion for each other was extreme. The entire story describes one of the most intensely pleasurable encounters possible between two people.

What is it then that I doubt? Well, it's simple, really. I doubt, in spite of the passion, tears, and professions of undying love, there is any connection between their passion and *the quality of their relationship in its entirety*. They have had a good day but that's about it. That's all you can say for sure. Tomorrow they may behave hatefully toward each other again. Simple logic tells us that frequent emotings in a relationship often imply frequent bad behavior (ultimately removed).

I have harped on this when discussing the emotion we call love and I shall harp on it more later. One of the reasons the emotion-called-love is not proof that a relationship is a good one, is that it shows up *every* single time in all human beings given the required circumstances. It is predictable and if you are to believe my formula, it can be created at will (instantaneously). Even couples with rotten relationships are capable of feeling the emotion-called-love. They may constantly beat on each other, cheat on each other, and swear they hate each other, yet when they break up, the fear of the future and the disruption of their time dependency creates an intolerable emotion. Then, after they make up, it's not long before things get back to normal. And need I remind you, normal is not good!

Would you believe the same thing happens with emotings? When lovers make up, kiss, and begin to cry (emote), they feel at that moment that they are in love. But—*those feelings truly mean nothing*. Don't misunderstand. We all seem to enjoy these feelings, but, as far as being able to trust them for guidance during life, *they can totally mislead us.*

Emotings are just too predictable. If screenwriters, politicians, ministers, and authors can cause the entire world to emote exactly when they want, what value do those feelings have? What do they tell us about the truths of life and relationships?

The logic involved in making life's decisions because we emote, could be compared to making those same decisions because our eyes dilate at some particular time or because we sweat at some particular time. My point is simply that these biological symptoms appear automatically and predictably because we are members of the human species.

We have to learn to ignore both emotions and emotings when they don't apply. When we experience an energy reaction as a result of some sort of threat to our survival, unless the threat is physical in nature (a real danger), we should do our best to make sure our behavior afterwards is reasonable. Expressing feelings of anger for example, is acceptable and serves to communicate with others, but succumbing to the anger and harming others in some fashion is not acceptable.

Similarly, staying in a relationship because we emote regularly isn't a wise approach. In both circumstances, our feelings misguide us.

Subtle Emotings

One final comment about the deceptive qualities of emotings: sometimes only one's intellect can catch them and see them for what they really are. The negative part of the formula that triggers emotings can be truly subtle—still negative, but so cunning it is difficult to pinpoint the exact trigger. Sometimes the reaction is triggered when a wish, desire or dream is fulfilled. Thus, if you have always *desired* to own a house and have *dreamed* about what it would be like, should someone suddenly step up and fulfill that dream by giving you your dream house, you would undoubtedly emote. So too would everyone else who watched it take place.

Currently there is a television show that does exactly this. The sponsors of the show rebuild a house to fulfill a family's dreams. Boy is that show ever a tearjerker! When the family is given the keys to the house, everyone watching cries. Of course, the show is very popular.

One of the best movies ever made that successfully caused viewers to emote is *Sleepless in Seattle*. The audience emotes several times during the movie because of a potential relationship between Sam (Tom Hanks) and Annie (Meg Ryan). We emote even though the two of them never actually meet until the final scene.

It took me a while to figure out what was causing the tears. I couldn't put my finger on the negative being removed whenever I caught myself emoting. Ultimately I decided they both longed for and passionately desired a perfect love relationship. The need for such a relationship is something most of us have felt, so when Sam and Annie get together in the end, it's as if we have all found our true love. Our loneliness and longing for love is vicariously removed. It is no wonder we cry.

There is an even slyer trigger out there; it occurs whenever *neutral and therefore not truly negative behavior* is suddenly made positive. When a husband who never seems to notice or care about his wife's needs suddenly surprises her with flowers, candy, and a night out on the town, she will surely emote at some point during the evening. His habitual indifference has unexpectedly been removed, which is why she emotes. Love will undoubtedly be expressed during her emotings.

There is a concept in behavioral psychology known as intermittent reinforcement and/or punishment. The advice given with this concept is to never be too consistent with either reinforcements or punishments. If you are, the person being reinforced or punished begins to *expect* the behavior from you and it loses its power. Without knowing this, the recipient of the reinforcement may not appreciate the original intent of the behavior.

That's as clear as mud, isn't it? To explain, let's elaborate on the husband story above. Suppose this man has a good friend down the street who is much better at pleasing his wife. In fact, this man would have to be called a great husband. He never forgets Valentine's Day, Mother's Day, his wife's birthday, etc. He always comes home with a gift or flowers to show her he loves her. But—because he is so consistent in this behavior—she *expects* the gifts. So, ho-hum, she never emotes when he gives them to her.

The sad part is, should he fail to remember an important date some year, he might end up in hot water for a few days. Why? Something good (the gifts and his positive behavior) has been removed—which is felt as punishment by his wife.

On the other hand, our less perfect husband can only improve on his circumstances. Since he rarely does expected things, whenever he miraculously does remember, he becomes "a wonderful husband."

> Those beloved "feelings" are the cause of massive self-deception.

Perhaps you can begin to see why I value Intellectual Love so highly. The normal expected behavior of humans isn't always that bright. Simple logic tells us to not behave in this manner. Why do we? Because we are taught to respond to life according to how we *feel*.

Truthfully, we need to be wary of our silly feelings in all circumstances in life.

Behavior First

For too many years I have watched people make life's major decisions based upon their feelings. The point I'm trying to make is that those beloved "feelings" are the cause of massive self-deception. Why do you think there are so many divorces? Why do you think most people are so confused about love? Why do you think mankind in general is always unhappy and discontented with life?

My hope is that by exposing the truth about love, people can make more intelligent decisions in the future. The bad feelings connected to emotions (anger, hatred, etc.) are obvious culprits. The devious emotings are another story. Since we like to emote, those feelings actually allow us to distort the truth to a greater degree. We are blinded by emotings and by the societal beliefs we learn as we grow up.

My conclusion: *"Nearly everything we have been taught about emotions is potentially false."* At the very least, false because of the confusion those beliefs cause.

A man came home from work one day to find his wife on the front porch with her bags packed.

"Just where the heck do you think you're going?" he asked.

"I'm going to Las Vegas," said the wife. "I just found out I can get $400 a night for what I give to you for free!"

The man said, "Wait a minute!" and then ran inside the house only to come back a few minutes later with his suitcases in hand.

"Where the heck are you going?" said the wife.

The man said, "I'm going with you. I can't wait to see how you're gonna live on $800 a year!"

CHAPTER 20

Maintaining Control:
The Problem With Emotings

"It is part of our pedagogy to teach the operation of thinking, feeling, and willing so that they may be made conscious. For if we do not know the difference between an emotion and a thought, we will know very little . . . We need to understand the components (of emotions) at work . . . in order to free their hold."

~ Mary Caroline Richards

I WAS WATCHING A MOVIE THE OTHER NIGHT WHEN A particular scene made me reflect upon the societal misunderstanding of emotings. One of the main characters in the story was a truly bad man. He had killed several people and was cruel and hateful to everyone. Yet, during a period of internal reflection he went through a moment of self-pity, at which point he began to emote. He cried like a baby for a few minutes—and his companion in the room did so too. It was a moving scene.

While he was emoting, I could imagine most viewers thinking to themselves: "Ah-h! He's not so tough! Deep down inside he has a good heart. He's merely putting on a tough-guy act." The assumption is that people who emote are good people "deep down inside."

I'm sure you can see what sort of foolish thinking this is. *Every human being on earth predictably emotes.* Emotings are a function of the autonomic (automatic) nervous system. If the conclusion were valid, we would all be kind, softhearted folks. I've met a few bad people, and kindness wasn't one of their virtues.

Thus, I repeat: emotings mean nothing!

Everyday Uses of Emotings

Much of human behavior can be tracked to this phenomenon of emoting. People have blindly followed leaders who have led them to their deaths. Religious "prophets" are professionals at the game. (Like good salesmen, they manage to acquire their fair share of cash and sex too.)

> It appears to me that much of a leader's "charisma" is directly tied to his ability to create periodic emotings in his followers.

It appears to me that much of a leader's charisma is directly tied to his ability to create periodic emotings in his followers. People essentially follow him because he "moved them emotionally."

I once listened to a gentleman give a speech that caused the audience to emote on several occasions. I watched while the people around me cried—even the men. Afterward, I asked a lady what she thought of the speech. She responded that it was great and he was "absolutely wonderful." Her enthusiasm was incredible. The point to be made here is that she thought *he* was wonderful. She never said anything definite about the content of the speech.

Later, when I thought about the speech, I concluded that the content was nothing unusual. He hadn't said anything that hadn't already been said by others many times in the past. His delivery and the particular stories he told made the difference.

The stories carried the day because emotings were connected to them. (By the way, the audience also bought a ton of books from him that night.)

Influencing The Masses

How much influence do you suppose emotings have on behavior? Obviously our love lives are seriously affected, but what about other possibilities? *I personally believe emotings significantly influence human behavior—more than we can possibly imagine.* These tears and touching sensibilities have changed the course of human history. Although emotings often bring people together, they can also strongly encourage an us-against-them syndrome.

I was watching a program about World War II the other day on the History Channel. The title of the presentation was *The Women of Germany.* At one point, it explained that Hitler could make thousands of German women (and men) cry like babies during his speeches. Later several of these women were interviewed and they remarked about how much Hitler was *loved* by everyone at the time.

Does this sound familiar? Make people emote and they will love you and follow you anywhere. I asked myself how anyone could manage to get an entire nation to emote in the first place? What negative was being removed? I can only speculate. Could it be that the defeat and subsequent shame of losing World War I literally set the German people up for mass emotings? Hitler merely removed the humiliation by declaring the German people to be the superior race. Any effective politician could have done so. Hitler wasn't really special. He was just there at the opportune time. I'll leave the conclusion to you.

Emotings: The Good versus the Dangerous

Scientifically, it seems apparent that emotings are designed to reward us for helping others overcome whatever problem they may be having. People feel better after having emoted. From a biological viewpoint, crying burns energy. Since most people are experiencing stress constantly, resulting in excess energy, they undoubtedly need to release as much energy as they can.

Emotings, then, are doubly rewarding—because of their *feel good* nature and because of their *feel better* nature.

Over the years I have learned to enjoy emoting. Whenever possible, I attend the so-called chick flicks, just to get in a good cry. While I enjoy the release, I am careful to treat emotings more intellectually than I did previously. They are simply good feelings—nothing more, nothing less.

After years of watching people emote under all sorts of circumstances, I have concluded that while emotings are generally positive feelings, they can have several unfortunate consequences. Some people seem to be addicted to the feelings and pursue them in all sorts of ways. Emotings appear to make people more gullible, more trustful, more vulnerable financially, more willing to believe in the unbelievable, and more easily manipulated to perform unethical types of behavior.

Perhaps the next goal for the scientific community should be to research and thoroughly understand these strange but wonderful feelings.

The greatest love is mother's love; after that comes a dog's love; after that the love of a sweetheart.
Polish Proverb

CHAPTER 21

True Emotions Summarized

"Everything that irritates us about others can lead us to an understanding of ourselves."

~ Carl Young

I MADE THE DISTINCTION BETWEEN EMOTINGS AND EMOTIONS so I could isolate the types of feelings that would fit one simple definition of *emotion* without others bleeding through and confusing the discussion.

Emotions are negative and emotings are positive. They are separate and distinct concepts. Of the two, emotions cause the greatest unhappiness to individuals but emotings add their share of disruptive behavior.

Emotions Simplified

Here are a few basic principles:

1. Whenever our physical, social, or psychological survival is threatened, we become *instantly* upset and, in reverse, whenever we experience one of those instantaneous energy reactions, *we have been threatened somehow.*

2. We acknowledge that what is taking place inside our bodies involves the production or conservation of

energy for the purpose of fighting or running from a perceived threat.

3. All instantaneous reactions in the body will simply be referred to as "energy reactions."

4. The uncomplicated word *upset* will be used to describe all energy reactions. The degree of upset we feel will be described relative to the amount of energy the body has produced. Thus, we might say we are a little upset or very upset, depending upon how high our blood pressure, heart rate, etc. went.

5. We realize the extra energy feels bad inside us and is seldom truly necessary for us to survive. It can and often does affect our behavior in a negative way.

6. We will do our best to ignore the internal energy production by not allowing it to affect our external behavior in an intellectually negative manner.

7. We will deal with the extra energy by burning it up through exercise. Singing, laughing, dancing, swimming, jogging, and similar activities will be used whenever necessary in order to return the body to a homeostatic balance.

8. Now that we know not to call the negative emotion *love*, we can stop making decisions because we think what we feel is love. Instead, we should use our intellect to make life's major decisions.

The dilemma with this process is that mankind has never been able to simply *ignore the energy*. Much of our everyday behavior can be understood by viewing it as an attempt to avoid things that cause energy reactions or behaving in some fashion while trying to rid the body of that energy.

For example, some people avoid giving speeches or attending cocktail parties because they are socially threatening and make them feel uncomfortable. (Even minor feelings of discomfort are caused by small amounts of "flight" energy.)

Similarly, people take medications and various other mind

altering drugs in order to cope with the stresses of life that have caused their bodies to produce too much extra energy.

Here is an interesting observation. Anthropologists have never found any society of mankind that didn't utilize mind-altering drugs. Whether those drugs are uppers, downers, or hallucinogenic in nature, doesn't seem to matter. *There is apparently an innate dissatisfaction with normal human existence* that creates a need to escape from reality. In my opinion, the escape is necessitated by energy reactions—since they are so numerous, odious, and debilitating.

> Of the two, emotions and emotings, emotions cause the greatest unhappiness to the individual.

Emotings Simplified

Here are some basic principles of emotings:

1. Whenever a negative circumstance is removed from our lives and/or the lives of others, we emote as a result.

2. While we can readily acknowledge that the feelings created by emotings are pleasant, they don't prove anything.

3. These positive feelings were created by nature in order to reward the individual for behaving in an unselfish fashion. The purpose was undoubtedly to keep us in groups for protection.

4. Since emotings can be produced in all people by the use of a simple formula, the person using the formula is not necessarily charismatic, wonderful, holy, or otherwise. While he could *possibly* be such, the proof is in his behavior—not in his ability to get people to emote.

5. Should we desire to experience emotings, we can do so by helping others when they are in need; taking care to do so intellectually.

6. Now that we know how emotings work, we can appreciate the feelings without basing our decisions on just those feelings. In fact, we need to be wary of all decisions made while under the influence of an emoting.

Emotings and Trust

For years I have speculated about what hormones and/or chemicals one would find during human emotings. My general conclusion has always been that emotings, since they are on the survival of the species side of the outline, would logically involve hormones similar to oxytocin, the cuddle hormone. I recently found evidence to support my supposition.

On June 1, 2005, researchers from the University of Zurich announced an astonishing discovery: When people inhale oxytocin, they react by becoming more trusting of other people. The oxytocin can easily enter the brain when sniffed, boosting social interactions like trust. In the June 2005 issue of the scientific journal, *Nature*, the researchers reported:

> "Oxytocin specifically affects an individual's willingness to accept social risks arising through interpersonal interactions . . . We find that intra-nasal administration of oxytocin causes a substantial increase in trusting behavior."

Based upon this research, there is a company that has made oxytocin available as a spray. The implied purpose would be to use the spray in order to "trick" people into trusting someone for monetary or other reasons. Sadly, it will undoubtedly work too, since, again, we have been taught to trust our feelings at all times.

The characteristics of emotings as delineated in this book, appear to have similar social consequences. Whether receiving oxytocin via a nasal spray or by way of a story that makes you cry, the affected individual appears to form a bond and to trust those involved at the time. Consequently, we should be wary of oxytocin in the future. Bonding with and/or trusting others should obviously be a function of the intellect; not one's feelings.

Emoting for Pleasure

Now it is time for you to write. I have a Website established to collect as many stories as possible that make people emote. The site is: www.Storiesthatmakeyoucry.com. If you know of a good story, either one you've heard, read, or written, that will make people cry, please e-mail it to me at Understandinglov @aol.com. I will post them on the Website. Then, whenever you need a good cry, you can log onto the site and sob away to your heart's content. Be sure to acknowledge and give credit to all known authors.

Coincidentally, a friend recently e-mailed the following story to me. It has been making the rounds on the Internet for at least a year. Since it makes most people emote, at least briefly, I'm including it. The originators tied it to some sort of religious belief, using it to prove a general religious point (which I have cut, since we know emotings don't prove anything).

So, here it is. I trust you will enjoy a good cry. No charge!

Kyle's Story

One day, when I was a freshman in high school, I saw a kid from my class walking home from school. His name was Kyle. It looked like he was carrying every single one of his schoolbooks. I wondered why anyone would want to carry all of his books home on a Friday. I could only conclude that he must really be a nerd.

As I was walking, I saw a bunch of kids running toward him. They ran at him, knocked his books out of his arms, and tripped him so he landed in the dirt. His glasses went flying. I saw them land in the grass about ten feet from him. As he looked up, I saw this terrible sadness in his eyes.

My heart went out to him, so I jogged over to him. I saw a tear in his eye as he crawled around looking for his glasses. As I handed them to him I said, "Those guys are jerks. They really should get lives."

He looked at me and said, "Hey, thanks!" There was a big smile on his face. It was one of those smiles that showed real gratitude. I helped him pick up his books and, as it turned out, he lived near me. I asked him why I had never seen him before. He replied that until recently he had gone to a private school.

173

I had never hung out with a private school kid before but I carried some of his books and we talked all the way home. He turned out to be a pretty cool kid. I invited him to play a little football with my friends, and he accepted.

We hung out all weekend and the more I got to know Kyle, the more I liked him. My other friends eventually felt the same.

Monday morning came and there was Kyle with that huge stack of books again. I stopped him and said, "Boy, you're gonna really build some serious muscles carrying those books every day!" He laughed and handed me half of them.

Over the next four years, Kyle and I became best friends. When we were seniors, we began to think about college. Kyle decided on Georgetown, and I chose Duke. In spite of being separated, I knew we would always be friends. The miles between us would never be a problem.

Because he actually was somewhat of a nerd, Kyle ended up being the valedictorian of our class and therefore had to prepare a speech for graduation. Even though I had always teased him about being a nerd, now I was glad it wasn't me having to get up there and speak.

On graduation day, Kyle looked great. He had really discovered himself during high school and had physically grown up and filled out. Now he actually looked good in glasses. He had also had more dates than I had during high school and truthfully all the girls loved him. Boy, sometimes I was jealous. Today was one of those days.

I could see that he was nervous about his speech, so I smacked him on the back and said, "Hey, big guy, you'll be great!"

He looked at me with one of those looks (the really grateful ones) and smiled.

He cleared his throat as he started his speech. "Graduation," he began, "is a time to thank those who have helped you make it through the tough times in life. Thanking your parents, your teachers, your siblings, maybe a coach but mostly—your friends. I am here to tell all of you that being a friend to someone is the best gift you can ever give him. I am going to tell you a story about my best friend: a friend who literally saved my life when we were kids."

I stared at my friend in disbelief as he told the story of that first day we had met. I had never known this before, but he had planned to kill himself over the weekend. He talked about how he had cleaned out his locker so his mom wouldn't have to do it later and was therefore packing his entire locker of stuff home. He looked straight at me and gave me a little smile.

"Thankfully," he continued, " I was saved. My friend saved me from doing the unspeakable."

I heard a gasp go through the crowd as this handsome, popular boy told everyone about his weakest moments. I saw his mom and dad looking at me and smiling that same grateful smile. Not until that moment did I realize its depth.

Never underestimate the power of your actions. With one small gesture you can change a person's life.

CHAPTER 22

Love's Trap:
Everyday Time Bombs

"Man's love is of man's life a thing apart, 'tis woman's whole existence."

~ Byron, Don Juan

IN THE FINAL ANALYSIS, LOVE IS CONFUSING BECAUSE IT IS SO complicated. So much is involved with the experience of love and the expressions related to that experience it is impossible to focus on any single aspect and do the topic justice. Love is more than any one of its parts, so even attempting to define it has historically proven fruitless. Yet, at times, we "feel" we know what it is. This book has been an attempt to analyze those feelings.

These feelings differ from relationship to relationship and can involve varying classes of feelings depending on the particular relationship. We have concluded that there are two major classes of feelings related to love: emotions and emotings. When people fall in love, they will undoubtedly experience both types of feelings at some point during the relationship. As we have concluded, one is wonderful; the other is potentially despicable.

When it comes to falling in love, the rule might be to simply *proceed with caution*. Too many people charge right in and establish a relationship with someone without considering whether or not a good match is possible.

An old adage states that opposites attract. While this may be somewhat true, similarities are better when it comes to long-lasting relationships. The more similar one is to one's partner, the more likely peace and harmony will reign. Opposing ideas, religious beliefs, opinions, desires, goals, etc. are breeding grounds for disagreement. Disagreement leads to unhappy, unpleasant feelings, which in turn lead to avoidance responses. (All negative emotions are simply avoidance responses at their core.)

Getting along becomes a chore and the relationship turns into work. Communication breaks down and no one enjoys life any longer. Don't allow yourself to become too time dependent on someone out of personal need, loneliness, or laziness. I use the word *laziness* because being romantically lazy can lead to time dependency. Once two people begin dating it is easy to drift aimlessly along while spending more and more time with the new companion. Why continue to look around when you have a convenient person available? Why? Because time dependency disrupted hurts—remember?

Whenever a relationship is fraught with emotion it signals trouble in the relationship. Emotion is created by disagreements. Disagreements occur when two people don't see eye to eye on a particular subject. If you start a relationship with even a beautiful but ill-matched person, you are headed for trouble. Consequently, while the passion and fun may be great for a while, if you aren't careful to control your time dependency, you may be crying yourself to sleep or drowning your sorrows with liquor—sooner rather than later.

Up to this point, all references to marital relationships have been to those wherein both people are either equally time dependent or time independent of each other. In reality, however, most marriages are built around circumstances that require one partner be more time dependent than the other. In some households, the husband goes to work every day while the wife stays home to keep house and care for the children. This lifestyle can lead to a time-dependent arrangement. (Realize that other lifestyles will result in a person's becoming too time dependent upon another. The fulltime housewife is simply a familiar example and can serve to help us understand time dependency more thoroughly.)

A woman who stays home and keeps house all day can expect to follow a routine that goes something like this:

1. Rise at 6:30 a.m. to prepare breakfast.
2. Send husband off to work and clean up the dishes.
3. Read newspaper while drinking a cup of coffee.
4. Put a load of clothes in the washing machine; then dig out the vacuum and start cleaning.
5. Pause to make a few phone calls.
6. Begin thinking about dinner and take some meat out of the freezer.
7. Fantasize about escape from this mundane existence.
8. Pause to nap (don't you wish).
9. Begin preparing dinner.
10. Greet husband, who is home from a hard day's work.
11. Serve dinner.
12. Do dishes.
13. Prepare for bed.
14. Make love with husband (optional).
15. Go to sleep while thinking about what to fix for breakfast.

(Note: If children become part of the routine, insert "pause to yell at kids," several hundred times during the schedule.)

Obviously, the description of this routine is an exaggeration, since many housewives are driving all over town doing errands and hauling kids everywhere imaginable. I wanted to use this exaggerated example, however, to make a few points.

Two major difficulties occur with this schedule. The first and most important problem with the arrangement is that many of these women communicate with absolutely no one else during their day. Their lives are taken up with their husbands (and children), making them very time dependent upon their family since just the family is satisfying all of her needs. One of the misfortunes of this arrangement is that, generally, many of her needs are not being satisfied by anyone.

I once knew a couple so totally in love it was embarrassing. Every time you'd see them, they would be hanging all over other each other, hugging and kissing. They couldn't get enough of each other. They had a two-year-old son so the wife stayed home every day while the husband went to work. He worked alone in an office so, of course, they were constantly on the phone talking to each other during the day. They were, in a nutshell, *extremely* time dependent on each other.

One day on his way to work he developed car trouble. In order to get help he had to hike a couple of miles. Consequently, he was a bit late getting to his office. His wife, however, had begun calling at the exact time she always did. When there was no answer she began to worry. She called a number of people looking for him. When they knew nothing, she panicked. By the time it was over she had called the police, the sheriff's department, the state patrol, and numerous others. He made it to work about an hour late, but the damage had been done. She showed up at his office fifteen minutes later and was a basket case. The tears flowed while she accused him of being inconsiderate and selfish. She insisted he should have called her. How he was supposed to have done so was not suggested. The fact he hadn't called was all that mattered to her.

The net result of this scene was that the embarrassed husband began to feel trapped by his wife's needy behavior and resentful of his obligation to constantly interact with her. They began having serious arguments about the future of their relationship. Ultimately, they ended up in marriage counseling.

I should point out that it isn't necessarily the lifestyle of a housewife that is to blame, since many women are happy being housewives. The main criterion for measuring its worth lies in the number of people (adults) the women encounter and relate to during the day. If the house is a hubbub of activity, with friends and relatives constantly going in and out, the housewife-lifestyle can be a happy one indeed.

The second difficulty with this lifestyle takes more explanation.

After several years of staying home and being under-stimulated, a housewife may feel discontented with her life. She might begin to make demands on her husband for more enter-tainment. In the meantime her husband, who has been out of the house and involved with the world all along, has had all of the excitement he can stand. The request to "do something exciting tonight" is met with resistance. As a result, a conflict develops between them that is difficult to resolve. Many broken marriages are made up of this combination. Inequities of time dependency can cause almost insurmountable difficulties.

It is predictable also that since the emotion-called-love is caused by threats to time dependency, whenever a husband disappoints his wife somehow (not getting home immediately after work, forgetting anniversaries, etc.), she will experience an acute emotional reaction.

Her husband, who has essentially *lost his time dependency* upon her (since he has been busy working), will seldom get upset about anything except for her unreasonable demands and illogical behavior.

The dilemma couples like this face is perplexing. Because of the imbalance of time dependency, disappointment, frustration, and resentment all become part of the relationship. The extremely time dependent partner will experience a great deal of frustration and disappointment whenever her plans are dis-rupted, while the time independent partner may begin to feel the other person is entirely too selfish, demanding, or hard to please. The independent partner states, "Nothing ever seems to please you. What happened to the happy person I married?"

If this pattern continues for any length of time, the quality of the relationship suffers severely.

Drawbacks to Time Dependency

Of all the possible combinations involving dating and marriage, the worst possible relationship is one in which one partner is time dependent upon his mate while the other is time independent. In this situation, all the drawbacks to time dependency are exaggerated for one person, while his mate does not suffer from the drawbacks.

If you get yourself into this type of relationship, you are asking for trouble. Let's look in a general sense at a few of the drawbacks to becoming time dependent upon someone, and why these problems are made worse if that person is not at least a little time dependent upon you in return.

1. Time dependency disrupted creates emotion and has insecurity as its partner. If your partner is a secure, unemotional individual, you will probably be on the bottom of the dog pile. Being in this position makes it easy for you to be controlled. (If you don't obey, your lover will leave you, period!) Instead of a husband or wife, you can become a victim. The first rule of the house is the old "when-I-snap-my-fingers-you-jump" routine. It is difficult to enjoy any relationship under such conditions.

2. What little security you do have can disappear instantly. This is made all the more serious since your partner may not get too upset if you are the one to leave. While you may be missed when you are gone, it will undoubtedly be short-lived. Thus, since it wouldn't bother your partner too much (emotionally, at least) if the relationship ended, the chances are even more likely it will end. In most cases, you would be doing most of the work trying to keep it together, because you need the relationship more. In contrast, two equally time dependent people will both work to keep things going because they both want the relationship.

3. At the very least, time dependency limits your horizons. By not being out and about with others, you get into a rut. This can make you a boring person. The problem is

that your busy partner may also become bored with you. People avoid that which is boring to them. Consequently, you may discover that your mate begins to avoid you.

4. Time dependency also prevents you from knowing what's going on around you. If you seldom come into contact with others, you are likely to be viewed as being, simply, "out of it." If your mate pictures you in the same light, you can actually be an embarrassment in social situations. The more time you spend with others in social situations, the more comfortable and fluent you become.

These are just a few of the drawbacks to time dependency that are magnified whenever the other partner is time independent. This sort of relationship is not a good idea—for either person. The best we can do to prevent debilitating emotions is to understand them and thereby learn to control and ignore them as best as we can. This can be accomplished in a love relationship by controlling time dependency in the first place.

> The best we can do in preventing debilitating emotions is to understand them and thereby learn to control and ignore them as best as we can.

Communication

Another serious drawback to an imbalanced time-dependent relationship relates to the problem of communication between two people. In essence, an imbalance of time dependency can actually break down and prevent effective communication in a relationship. A time-independent person must be careful about what he says and does around his lover because many comments and activities that should be indifferent and unimportant can be misunderstood and misinterpreted by his time-dependent mate. A time-independent wife, for example, who makes the mistake of pointing out how good-looking another man is, is asking for trouble. Consequently, and this is the whole point, she must keep such thoughts to herself in order to prevent the crisis that might develop. In fact, any potentially threatening thought she might have or action she might perform must be concealed from her mate, and since so many things can easily threaten a time-dependent mate, the result is that the two of them don't know as much about each other as they should.

Let's consider a situation that happens all the time. The star of this story will be Lucy. Lucy is in love with a man named Clint, and Clint is in love with her. Everything is peaches and cream until the "villain" enters the scene. The villain is a man named Bart, who meets Lucy on the beach one day and strikes up a conversation with her. Poor Lucy! She knows she is in love with Clint, but here is this gorgeous hunk of a man actually talking to her. Oh, well! Clint won't care, will he? Well, one thing leads to another and the entire afternoon simply disappears—one that Lucy enjoyed very much.

Now here's my point. Can Lucy tell Clint about her wonderful afternoon? Maybe, maybe not! It depends on many variables. Ideally she should be able to share her experiences with the man she loves, who would be gloriously happy for her and encourage her to continue being engaging and outgoing in the future. (Admittedly this does happen on occasion.)

However, the majority of people wouldn't even consider mentioning the experience to their partners. Thus, they begin to conceal things from each other—things about themselves, their beliefs, and their behavior that eventually, when hidden, begin to build a barrier between them that becomes harder to surmount as the years go by.

And here's something else that's sad. Lucy may actually tell her best friend about the experience with Bart. The friend will share the experience with Lucy and, therefore, will know more about Lucy than Clint does. It's too bad that a person's best friend is often more accepting of one's behavior and beliefs than the person who is in love with him.

The difference is in the time dependency. Because Lucy's relationship with Bart didn't threaten her relationship with her best friend, she was able to share the experience with her friend. On the other hand, the time Lucy spends thinking and talking about Bart takes away from her level of time dependency on Clint. This could threaten Clint and, more importantly, the relationship she has with him.

This is not to suggest, of course, that time-independent couples are always capable of tolerating such behavior; however, it would seem that they should be much more able to do so. One of the main differences between the reactions of time-dependent and time-independent people is often merely one involving the level of the feelings or emotions that occur under conditions such as this.

If Clint were to be extremely time dependent upon Lucy, he may become so upset that he will do something irrational and possibly aggressive. On the other hand, his reactions will not be severe if he is not too time dependent upon her. While he may be a little upset with Lucy, he may not *feel* that way inside and there is a huge difference between the two perceptions.

This discussion is not made to suggest that an imbalanced time-dependent relationship can't work at all—because it can. It does point out, however, that such an alliance is fraught with obstacles and is, therefore, much more difficult to maintain over long periods. It requires much more work.

One advantage of marriage it seems to me is that when you fall out of love with him or he falls out of love with you it keeps you together until maybe you fall in again.
                    Judith Viorst

Chapter 23

Emotionless Love:
Loving For the Pleasure of it All

"Love moderately; Long love doth so."
~ Shakespeare, Romeo and Juliet

THERE ARE MORE BENEFITS TO TIME INDEPENDENCE THAN THE lack of emotional trauma. In marriage, for example, because two individuals with two separate personalities live together for long periods of time, problems develop that have nothing to do with love. Some of the major areas of difficulty in situations involving cohabitation are personal habits, sex, work-load, and money. Obviously the more time two people spend together; the more likely it is these areas can create strains in the relationship.

If Miss Ragamuffin marries Mr. Clean, it is ten times more difficult to live in peace and harmony if they are constantly together. In all likelihood, under these circumstances Miss Ragamuffin will eventually get on Mr. Clean's nerves because of, for example, her habit of brushing her teeth and splashing the bathroom mirror at the same time. In reverse, Mr. Clean can become intolerable to Miss Ragamuffin with his habit of playing the stereo at ten decibels above sanity while he continuously vacuums the floor. The more time people spend together the more likely problems will develop between them.

It is easy to make light of these problems and to dismiss them as being insignificant. However, in all probability, most problems in marriages begin in connection with these little difficulties. A slight disagreement over the toothpaste can lead to anger over the stereo. Anger over the stereo can lead to aggression and tears. All of which can lead to unhappiness and divorce.

Relating this back to time dependency, it should be apparent that time independence requires that a married couple spend less time together. Instead of being together for up to a possible twenty-four hours each day, they are together for perhaps ten hours at the most; e.g., from nine p.m. to seven a.m. Even time-independent couples that don't spend time together may still be time dependent upon each other. This is possible whenever they aren't getting their needs satisfied by others when they are apart.

One of the other less obvious benefits to time independence centers around the fact that even the best of us can be a bore under the right circumstances. People who are time independent have two advantages here. First, since they encounter numerous people every day, they have a good chance of learning and experiencing many things. This has the effect of making them less boring to their partner. People who are not constantly together may spend many interesting hours sharing the experiences they have had while they were separated.

The second advantage time-independent people have is they aren't as likely to get on each other's nerves when they are together. People who are time dependent can find themselves with nothing to say to each other because everything has been discussed already. After several years of being together, it is possible for each person to predict exactly what his mate will say under most circumstances. In fact, they can even tell each other's favorite stories verbatim (right down to clearing their throats precisely as their mates do just before the punch line). Thus, while it is true that the emotion-called-love may always be present in their relationship, the much more important factor of pleasure that each is receiving from the relationship may be slowly diminishing.

Obviously, every marriage or relationship is unique in its own right. Time independence in and of itself is no magic formula for happiness and, in truth; too much time independence can cause problems too.

Problems with Time Independence

Three main problem areas always seem to crop up whenever a couple attempts to organize their relationship in a time-independent fashion. They are indifference, jealousy, and insecurity.

Time-independent couples experience less emotional involvement with their mates and, as a consequence, may appear to be indifferent toward each other and may be so if they fail to consider their situation intellectually. It takes a straight-forward, logical, practical person to realize that the emotion-called-love is unrelated to the level of pleasure one receives from a relationship. In explaining this idea, I always state that the normal mind-body connection must be reversed.

> Intellectual love is truly the ideal love because it involves a commitment to each other.

In the normal love relationship, the body controls the mind; emotion controls intellect. People who think they are in love are continually doing things even they know are foolish. A distraught lover may phone his lost love at three o'clock in the morning, knowing full well that doing so will only make matters worse. The feelings he is experiencing have taken control over his intellect, and irrational behavior is the result.

In a time-independent relationship that is essentially void of emotion, the mind must remain in control. The intellect must face the relationship straight away and decide whether love is present or not. If a couple likes each other, then they must love each other; if they enjoy each other, then they must love each other. Thus, they can intellectually decide they are in love and, as a consequence, they can also intellectually decide they will stay together. I believe this type of Intellectual Love is stronger than Emotional Love ever will be. Intellectual love is truly the ideal love because it involves a commitment to each other.

Jealousy

The second problem time-independent couples encounter involves what I call "intellectual jealousy." I call it intellectual jealousy because it is only a property of the mind; very little emotional jealousy is involved. It is best exemplified by a comment a young woman made while we were talking about her time-independent relationship with her husband. She said something like this, "I don't really care what he does when he isn't with me; I just worry about whom he might be with, that's all."

This contradictory comment exemplifies the concerns of many time-independent couples. While they don't get as upset as most people do about love and they don't emotionally care to a level that others do, nonetheless, they realize their mates might find someone to replace them during their wanderings. From a mathematical approach, in fact, the probability that they might encounter someone to their liking is fairly good. The more people they encounter, the better those odds become. The possibility of being replaced creates the insecurity.

This dilemma is predictable. Even a time-independent person isn't totally independent if he has a love relationship with someone. By necessity, that relationship must be satisfying some needs. Thus, since needs are related to survival, whenever the satisfaction of those needs is threatened, the brain will at least take note of the situation. This causes the concerns the woman above expressed. It is only natural it should happen. These concerns are sometimes felt as insecurity, which is the third problem time-independent couples encounter.

All three of these problems, indifference, jealousy and insecurity, are best handled by our savior and superstar—Intellectual Love. The lines of communication should be kept open at all times, and the concerns of both partners should be discussed. As a result of these discussions, an intellectual agreement should be reached. It might go something like this:

> First of all, it shall be agreed that we two do, indeed, love each other. Therefore, be it resolved that as long as we continue to enjoy each other's company, as long as we continue to give each other pleasure, as long as we continue

to live a satisfying life in general, then we will mutually agree that we shall not leave each other for any reason. And, be it further resolved that, in the event that the pleasure and satisfaction being derived from this relationship should in any way be diminished, that fact shall be made known to the other person so that it can be dealt with accordingly.

Reassurance is the safest way to prevent difficulties in love. The need for security demands that we know where we stand with our mates. Not knowing our status creates more obstacles to happiness. By simply sticking to this agreement, a *commitment* is created that has more power than the word *love*. A promise to commit oneself to another seems more reassuring. Another great quote about love states that love is simply a decision—a decision to stay with a loved one at all costs.

Time Dependency and Health

Time dependency in old age suffers from the same drawbacks as time dependency in one's youth. However, old age has an even more serious drawback: Given the right circumstances, time dependency can kill you. Older people whose health is questionable in the first place are risking their lives if they allow themselves to become too time dependent on their mates. How many of us have heard it said that some older man or woman followed his mate to the grave? From the perspective of time dependency, such a course of action is to be expected.

The emotion connected to love is actually called many different things, and one of the words used to describe it is *grief*. The essential connotative difference between love and grief is that grief signals a death has occurred. Actually, any time we lose someone we love, we could say we grieve the loss. However, we don't refer to most losses as resulting in grief because the concept of grief is reserved for the relationship between love and death. Thus, since we know that excessive grief can lead to one's demise and the intensity of that grief is determined by the level of one's time dependency upon the person who has died, it again seems only practical that we control time dependency as we grow older.

Guided by these thoughts, we would be wise to do whatever

we can to help older people decrease their time dependencies, and then attempt to arrange our own lives in such fashion as to guarantee we will not be alone in our declining years and that we will always be involved with many other people and many activities in general.

HOW DO YOU DECIDE WHOM TO MARRY?

You got to find somebody who likes the same stuff. Like, if you like sports, she should like it that you like sports, and she should keep the chips and dip coming.

Alan, age 10

No person really decides before they grow up who they're going to marry. God decides it all way before, and you get to find out later who you're stuck with.

Kirsten, age 10

WHAT DO MOST PEOPLE DO ON A DATE?

Dates are for having fun, and people should use them to get to know each other. Even boys have something to say if you listen long enough.

Lynnette, age 8 (isn't she a treasure)

On the first date, they just tell each other lies and that usually gets them interested enough to go for a second date.

Martin, age 10 (wise beyond his years)

IS IT BETTER TO BE SINGLE OR MARRIED?

I don't know which is better, but I'll tell you one thing. I'm never going to have sex with my wife. I don't want to be all grossed out.

Theodore, age 8

It's better for girls to be single but not for boys. Boys need someone to clean up after them.

Anita, age 9 (bless you child)

HOW WOULD YOU MAKE A MARRIAGE WORK?

Tell your wife that she looks pretty, even if she looks like a truck.

Ricky, age 10

CHAPTER 24

Love's Independence:
Ignoring Raw Emotion

"You who seek an end to love, be busy and you will be safe."

~ Ovid

WHAT CAN ONE DO ABOUT TIME DEPENDENCY? WHY IS TIME dependency so intimately tied to our deepest feelings and emotions? How do you achieve time independence? Is time independence a desirable state of existence? Is an intimate, warm, caring relationship more important than worrying about some future state of unhappiness?

One of the final issues I want to address involves the question of how a person actually becomes time independent.

The simplest way to attempt to become time independent and thus more secure is to force yourself out of your present physical position and seek companionship from others. This is done, for example, by joining organizations and clubs where you can encounter other people and hopefully establish new friendships.

The following is a list of some of the things you can do that should lead to new relationships with other people.

191

1. Find a job in which you will be working with other people on a daily basis. Usually coworkers establish friendships and then spend time together away from the job.

2. Start a business of some sort, especially one that requires you to deal with the public. If nothing else, this will end your boredom.

3. Look for organizations (hospitals, churches, etc.) that need volunteers. This works well for the simple reason that these people need you, and as a consequence, they will be friendlier toward you from the beginning.

4. Apply for membership in social groups that entail activities you find interesting.

5. Get involved in athletics.

6. Go back to school.

7. Get out of the house! Period!

I once made these suggestions to a young housewife who was lonely and unhappy because her husband's job required him to be out of town frequently. Her remark was that if she had to become a "joiner" in order to meet people, perhaps she would rather stay home instead. My response was that if she had any hope of getting herself out of the depression she was in, she simply *must* do some of these things. *She* had to be the one to seek new friends because no one was going to seek her.

Another woman in a similar situation, except she also had two children at home, said she couldn't afford to do any of these things since she didn't have money to pay a baby-sitter for watching her children. My response was that she couldn't afford not to do so. If money was the issue, look for a job that would at least pay the baby-sitter. Just breaking even is better than nothing. Not only was her marriage at stake, but also her happiness and that of her children.

This might sound as if I am only interested in the problem of housewives. Actually, that is not the case. Men have as many problems with time dependency as women do. Anyone who fits the description should take heed of this discussion.

If you have tried to do some of these things in order to find new friends and have failed in the endeavor, it might be necessary for you to seek professional counseling. Knowing how to be sociable and likable is a talent that can be learned. If you didn't learn the formula as a young child (because you were raised time dependently), you can still learn.

I know that somewhere in the Universe exists my perfect soul mate—but looking for her is much more difficult than just staying at home and ordering another pizza.
Alf Whit

CHAPTER 25

The End of Love:
Facing The Future With Self-Awareness

"No matter how you look at it, all the emotions connected with love are not really immortal; like all other passions in life, they are bound to fade at some point. The trick is to convert love into some lasting friendship that overcomes the fading passion."

~ Harold Pinter

PERHAPS IT IS UNFORTUNATE THAT MANY RELATIONSHIPS END. Perhaps though, it is how things should be. Should the goal of life be to establish a love relationship with someone and then maintain it until death? In the past that might have made sense —but does it work today? Why especially, when marriages end, do people actually feel like failures? Where is it written that love should last forever?

Logic tells us that all of the glorified ideals about love are impossible to live up to. Why then do we beat ourselves up so much when things don't go perfectly in our love lives?

I caught a series on the History Channel a while back about the Roman Empire. One comment was intriguing. The historian stated that the average life expectancy at the time was twenty to twenty-five years. No wonder the religious leaders of the time expected people to stay together "until death do us part." Until death do us part might only have been five or ten years. That sounds a whole lot easier to accomplish than nowadays. If a couple were to marry at age twenty today and still be alive at age eighty, they would have to stay together for sixty years. That's a bit tougher. Maybe our expectations are just too high.

Can anyone who has reached fifty years old claim to be the same person he was at age twenty? It is doubtful. Some of us change so much, the twenty-year-old we were wouldn't even like the fifty-year-old we became. So how can we then expect to love another for the same period of time? Or someone to love us for the same period of time?

A number of years ago, during one of my seminars, a twice-divorced woman in her forties became irritated by the "arrogant smugness" of the happily married couples in the room. She challenged them to "just wait." Eventually they would realize how hard it is to stay together forever. Her first marriage had lasted thirteen years and she bragged that the first twelve were almost perfect. However, once she and her husband began to disagree about how to deal with one of their children, everything fell apart. Her second marriage was a mistake from the beginning, so the only thing for her to do was to end it quickly.

I tell her story because she believed there were more unhappily married couples in the world than happy ones. She claimed if she were to walk down any street in the country with a lie detector and ask everyone if they were happily married, the majority of them would have to say no. She stated that most people were just putting on a good show whenever they were out in public. Behind closed doors, things were different. From her perspective, all relationships seemed to eventually develop problems.

If you have lost or are about to lose a once-satisfying relationship, it is important to realize that life goes on. Look at the changes in your life as opportunities, not failures. Once you rearrange your life and become comfortable in a new one, you will feel better with each passing day. Follow the principles in this book and keep busy with things you enjoy. Look for the joyful aspects of life rather than dwelling on the negatives.

A Quick Review

When major changes occur in our lives, we are often forced out of our comfortable, safe and generally predictable routines. The primitive area of the brain doesn't take kindly to such events. From the moment our "boats get rocked" until we have successfully re-established a new comfort zone, our bodies will be full of extra energy to fight or run from the unwanted dangers.

To put that into plain English, when relationships end, we are often forced to move out of our homes, to find new friends, to fight with attorneys and former lovers, etc. The extra energy may be useful under those circumstances; but its presence makes us feel awful.

Old habits die hard, so even after reading this book, most people will call those energetic feelings love, depression, anger, hatred, sadness, anxiety, jealously, or of course, heartbreak. However, describing one's feelings using emotional words tends to confuse us and make us act foolishly. We often say and do things that are plain stupid.

My point is that we aren't necessarily depressed or angry, we are simply feeling the normal effects of having too much energy in our bodies. Believing anything else is potentially dangerous to one's physical and social well-being.

Suppose Jane, the mother of two, has been abandoned by her husband. He has left her with little money, no job, and no immediate way to pay the bills each month. Consequently, it is absolutely predictable that her body will be filled with too much energy. Her future and that of her children is definitely being threatened, so from that perspective her brain is responding logically. If, however, she can simply realize that her feelings are merely symptoms of excess energy, she might begin to jog in the mornings in order to burn off the extra energy.

In contrast, if she decides her feelings are those of anger, she might instead try to destroy her husband's car or personal belongings. She could be inclined to do so because she grew up learning that angry people behave in that fashion. In our society it would be considered normal to do so.

If she decides her feelings are those of depression, she might allow herself to stay in bed all day and to ultimately take an overdose of sleeping pills because that is what depressed people do. So, instead of saying, "I am depressed" to herself (giving her permission to eat too much, drink too much, sleep all day, yell at everyone around her, miss work, commit suicide, and so forth) it is more constructive to simply exercise her bad feelings away.

The same applies to the other emotional labels. Any life-threatening situation follows the same course. Looking at everything from the energy approach allows us to deal with our problems in a more intelligent and constructive fashion.

Jane needs to work hard to rearrange her life. Establishing a new daily routine is critical because without a routine of some sort, her brain will constantly produce extra energy, keeping her continuously upset. Even a much less satisfying routine is better than the feared unknown.

When Jane is required to move out of a beautiful house into an apartment, the sooner this task is accomplished the better. Once a new, predictable routine is established, her brain will relax and stop upsetting her. Doing so may not be easy, but hopefully family and friends will help her through the current crisis.

Finally, considering what we have covered in this book, it is important for Jane to realize that her time-dependent feelings are not connected to any love she might feel for her husband. While she may still love him—her current feelings are not evidence of that. If her husband was an all-around great guy, there might still be reasons to love him because being with him gives her a great deal of pleasure. Still, the emotions can't be allowed to force her back to him if getting back with him isn't the best for all concerned.

No matter what happens, staying in control is vitally important. Time will pass and time is famous for healing wounds. Behaving well and intelligently has its rewards, too. Someday, things will improve and a positive relationship with an ex-husband can be invaluable, especially for the kids.

People shop for a bathing suit with more care than they do a husband or wife. The rules are the same. Look for something you'll feel comfortable wearing. Allow for room to grow.
Erma Bombeck

CHAPTER 26

Take Control of Your Love Life

"Know thyself."

~ Socrates

TAKING CONTROL OF YOUR LOVE LIFE AND LIFE IN GENERAL ARE closely tied together. Now that some of the mysteries of love have been exposed, many more mysteries about living a happy, contented life are within your grasp. Hopefully some of the ideas in this book will make a difference to you.

Sexual, Attachment, and Intellectual Love are the basis of good relationships. Fostering and nurturing them, once found, is wise.

For example, if sex is vitally important to satisfying relationships, why then do we allow it to die so easily? I am well aware that nature has somehow set it up to do so, but I doubt we are helpless. Once the initial passion diminishes, should we allow ourselves to stop showing affectionate touching behavior toward our lovers? How hard is it to make it a point to kiss and cuddle, even without the original passion? It's not hard at all and if purposefully done, relationships would continue to thrive.

In the same vein, how hard is it to be kind and considerate toward each other whenever possible? Instead of allowing the selfish person in us to surface, shouldn't we do our best to stifle him? Controlling emotionally driven impulses prevents misunderstandings and keeps disagreements civil. If you are currently involved in a relationship you think is worth keeping, perhaps it is time to discuss this book in order to clear up any misunderstandings. Then, once you are able to pinpoint the main source of friction, work as a team to correct the problems.

If, for example, your relationship is a good one in many ways but money problems are causing too much tension, doesn't it make sense to tackle the money problems by looking to experts for advice? Money problems create energy reactions we typically label as being worry or anxiety. Anxiety gives you permission to misbehave toward others and to blame others for how you feel inside (lousy, of course). Thus, rather than getting control of your own spending habits or exercising the bad feelings away, you instead take your unhappiness out on the most available person—your spouse.

What I have consistently maintained throughout this book, is that we give our *feelings* way too much credibility—all day, every day. What is going on inside our bodies shouldn't be allowed to surface and cause foolish behavior. As we have ascertained, many feelings previously called love are unpleasant ones. Exposing the truth should create better relationships.

It is my belief that *awareness* of the workings of both emotings and emotions can allow you to control your reactions to them. Extending the awareness to both partners in a relationship and discussing the concepts will work. Thus, I suggest you share this book with the person you love.

There are two points I hope you will seriously contemplate. The first is that love is not an emotion. One of the areas of life where this thought can make a substantial difference involves that of deciding whether or not to get married or divorced because of the emotion-called-love. I hope you now understand emotion is only indirectly related to love, since it is caused by time dependency, which isn't an accurate barometer for love (of pleasure).

If you are involved with someone and are therefore periodically emotional in connection with that person, you should not decide to get married because of that emotion. Instead, your decision should be determined practically, according to how well you are matched and how well you get along with each other generally. If you are constantly fighting and bickering before marriage, no matter how strong your emotions and emotings might be, you will undoubtedly continue to fight after marriage. You can't marry someone who mistreats you or is cruel toward you because such a relationship is not guaranteed to improve after marriage.

There is a lot of talk about "finding your one and only true love." But it should be apparent, if you judge love from the perspective of emotion, *you will fall in love with anyone you let yourself become time dependent upon.* The emotion shows up every time, in every relationship, after time dependency is established. Thus, you can't allow emotion to control your decision about marriage and your future life.

Sure, if the person you are in love with is a kind and considerate person who always treats you respectfully, it is possible that he or she will make a great marriage partner. But even then, other factors should influence your decision. Your age, your economic status, your respective religious beliefs, etc.—all of these things should be treated practically and discussed logically. There is no rush to get married anyway, is there?

Remember this also: in many breakups, two decent people are involved. Most people try to be reasonable and considerate. It just doesn't always look that way. Generally, the breakups occur because they simply weren't matched well to begin with.

Finally, remember that every human experiences energy reactions and all people emote—but that does not determine whether or not they are good people. *Feelings plus flowery talk mean nothing.* Only a person's behavior determines his goodness. Don't be fooled by other things. It really doesn't matter how nice a person sounds, how beautiful he looks, how concerned he acts, even how "holy" he seems. The proof is in his behavior. If someone claims, for example, to love everyone but continually acts unethically, his behavior gives him away. Words and feelings are hollow indeed. Actions speak louder! Put this in your head for the rest of your life!

A person's behavior is all that counts in life.
And that, dear reader, is especially true in one's love life.

Good luck and good loving!

Chapman, Gary. *The Five Love Languages: How to Express Heartfelt Commitment to Your Mate.* Moody Publishers, 1996.

Fischer, Helen. *Why We Love: The Nature and Chemistry of Romantic Love,* Henry Holt and Company, New York, 2004.

Montagu, Ashley. *Touching: The Human Significance of the Skin,* Columbia University Press, New York and London, 1971.

Schlessinger, Dr. Laura. *The Proper Care and Feeding of Husbands,* Harper Collins, New York, 2004.

Wilson, Edward O. *On Human Nature,* Harvard University Press, Cambridge, Mass. and London, England, 1978.

INDEX

Visit **www.mystiqueoflove.com**

or phone **970-669-1801** to order

additional copies of this book and to find

information on upcoming classes and

speaking engagements.